FOR
PEOPLE
—AND—
FOR
PROFIT

FOR PEOPLE
—AND
FOR PROFIT

A Business Philosophy for the 21st Century

Kazuo Inamori

Translated by T. R. Reid

KODANSHA INTERNATIONAL LTD.
Tokyo ▪ New York ▪ London

Distributed in the United States by Kodansha America, Inc., 114 Fifth Avenue, New York, New York 10011, and in the United Kingdom and continental Europe by Kodansha Europe Ltd., 95 Aldwych, London WC2B 4JF.

Published by Kodansha International Ltd., 17-14 Otowa 1-chome, Bunkyo-ku, Tokyo 112 and Kodansha America, Inc. Originally published in Japanese under the title of *Atarashii Nihon, atarashii keiei,* copyright © 1994 by Kazuo Inamori. English translation copyright © 1997 by Kodansha International Ltd. All rights reserved. Printed in Japan. First edition, 1997

97 98 99 10 9 8 7 6 5 4 3 2 1
CIP data available.

ISBN 4-7700-2030-9

Contents

Translator's Preface: About Kazuo Inamori   9

PART 1: MY VIEW OF JAPAN

Chapter 1. The Japanese System: Back to Square One   19
    Faceless Japan
    The *Mura* Theory: Village Society
    It Is Time to Change Our Values

Chapter 2. Why Japanese Business Is Criticized
  Around the World   30
    The Result of Market-Share Mania
    Japan's Self-righteous Companies
    Learning from Traditional Market Law
    Why Creativity Isn't Valued
    Management That Stresses Personality

Chapter 3. Living in a Global Society   46
    The Philosophy of Circulation and Regeneration
    The Wisdom of African Hunters
    Slash-and-Burn Farming
    Coexistence and the Regenerative Cycle
    Living Together in Society
    Philanthropy and a Respect for a Plurality of Values
    Coexistence in a Global Society

PART 2: CORPORATIONS IN SOCIETY

Chapter 4. The Need for Corporate Self-Control   61

    What We Learn from Nature
    From a Closed Corporate Society to an Open One
    Fair Corporate Management Through Openness
    Independent Small Businesses Will Change Japan
    Toward Management That Satisfies the Public

Chapter 5. The Role of the Government   75

    Public Administration for the Public
    A Bureaucratic System Puts Bureaucrats First

Chapter 6. Creating a Truly Free Society   87

    Fixing the Price Gap to Improve the Quality of Life
    Let's Deregulate—and Leave the Decisions to the Public
    From Bureaucracy to Independence
    Toward a Genuine Democracy
    Spreading the Spirit of Social Harmony Worldwide

PART 3: MANAGEMENT FROM THE HEART

Chapter 7. Good Motives and Selfish Motives   103

    The Material and Emotional Fulfillment of Employees
    The Challenge of the Telecommunications Industry
    Moving into Cellular Communications

Chapter 8. Eleven Key Concepts for Effective
  Management   115

Chapter 9. The Way of the Manager   128

    The Way of the Leader

PART 4: MY THEORY OF HUMANITY

Chapter 10. Fate and Human Will   139
Strong Willpower
Fate is Affected by Good Thoughts
Elevating Your Mental Dimension
A Formula for Life

Chapter 11. Creating a Spiritual Dimension   154
The Changeable and the Unchangeable Spirit
Our Souls Indicate Where Happiness Lies

Chapter 12. Caring for Others   161
The Difference between Heaven and Hell
Concern for Others Expands Your Horizons
Make Concern for Others the Basis of Your Actions
Extending the Spirit of Concern for Others
Living a Life of Self-Awareness
The Kyoto Prizes

THE REFORM OF JAPAN   177

The Realities of Japan's Political System
Issues in the Financial and Industrial Sectors
Government by Bureaucrats, Not by Law
The Protection of Producers and Suppliers
The Selfishness of Private Corporations
A Pragmatic Approach to Reform
The Kyoto Mayoral Election
Changing Japan's Political System

Translator's Preface:
About Kazuo Inamori

For the great corporations of the Western world, the 1990s have proven to be an era of bitter political controversy. With "efficiency" the watchword and "competitiveness" the goal, corporate managers in the United States and Europe have embarked on campaigns of sweeping change—change that has not always been welcomed outside the boardroom. Whether it is called "restructuring," "re-engineering," or "downsizing," this drive for lean management has sparked a furious backlash. Business leaders who once enjoyed the title "good corporate citizens" now open the newspaper to find themselves labeled "ruthless," "brutal," and "killers." According to the *Wall Street Journal*, the chairman of AT&T became such a social pariah after a round of massive layoffs that the company had to mount a major public relations effort with the aim—so far, unsuccessful—of restoring his reputation.

Critics in the media and the political world—many of them completely lacking in business experience—have insisted that large-scale downsizing and job reductions are not necessary to achieve efficiency and competitiveness. "There must be," these critics say, "another way." In this book, one of the world's most successful business managers argues that there is, indeed, another way to corporate success.

As he describes here, Kyocera Corporation's Kazuo Inamori has built a series of intensely competitive, highly profitable companies without relying on such strategies. Indeed, he has staked much of his career on a commitment to putting employees and their families first. He has battled it out with major competitors in industrial markets around the world—while striving, with an almost religious fervor, to be fair and square with his employees, his customers, and even his competitors. And he has made it all work to the benefit of stockholders as well. That explains why this book, setting forth the Inamori philosophy of management, was such a success in Japan—and why the appearance of an English version seems so timely right now.

If a book espousing Inamori's principles were to be written by a liberal politician or a left-wing activist, it would be easy to ignore. However, Inamori's ideas are not quite so simple to brush aside, for he has used these principles as the foundation for a stunningly successful business empire. Kazuo Inamori is the founder and chairman of Kyocera, a Kyoto-based maker of ceramics (hence "Kyocera") that has become a global leader in a wide variety of high-tech products, ranging from semiconductor packages and electronic components to photovoltaic solar cells and optical equipment.

Despite competition from companies throughout the world, Kyocera still enjoys a global market share greater than 60 percent in several product lines that are essential for modern semiconductor-based electronics. He is also the founder of Daini Denden (DDI), the first long-distance telephone company to challenge Japan's long-time communications monopoly, NTT (Nippon Telegraph and Telephone Corporation). DDI, too, has been a major success, particularly since its advance into the booming cellular telephone business. With these two, and a few smaller companies acquired along the way, Inamori's companies have global sales close to US$15 billion (¥1.5 trillion).

Inamori has also emerged as one of Japan's leading corporate philanthropists—and this in a country with almost no tradition of individual philanthropy. He is equally famous in his home country as an outspoken critic of the business establishment and the bureaucracy. Indeed, those Americans who have been complaining for years about closed markets and closed-minded government ministries in Japan will find a kindred spirit in the pages of this book. It's likely that Western trade negotiators will be quoting Inamori for a long time to come.

It is one thing, of course, to start from scratch and build a family of multibillion-dollar global companies. It is one thing to come up from near-poverty and build a large personal fortune. It is one thing to challenge long-established governmental and social structures. But in Japan it is something else entirely when they start writing comic books about you. And Kazuo Inamori received that honor a few years back, when the comic-book version of his biography, *Kyocera no chosen* ("The Kyocera Challenge") was published. In a sense, Inamori's story fits the format well, for it is a dramatic tale of achievement against the odds.

Born in 1932, Inamori battled disease and various family problems as a youth. He kept flunking the entrance exams for prestigious schools, and finally went from an undistinguished high school to a little-known university in his home town of Kagoshima, on the southern tip of Kyushu, the southern island of Japan. After rejections from other companies, he finally managed to land a job at Shofu Kogyo, a small insulator company in Kyoto, Japan's ancient capital.

The era—it was the mid-1950s—was an important moment in the ceramics industry worldwide. The emergence of television as a mass-market product had created the need for a new kind of electric insulator to support the electron gun at the base of the picture tube. Normal insulators could not do the job; a new type of ceramic material might, if mixed and sintered properly, but it was a difficult product to make, and Shofu refused to take the need seriously. Inamori, increasingly despondent about his firm's unwillingness to act, eventually did something thoroughly un-Japanese: he quit.

With borrowed money and a line of credit secured by an acquaintance who put up his house as collateral, he started Kyocera in 1959. He brought with him seven other ceramics engineers from Shofu, and the following year hired thirteen people. Two years later he took on another eleven recent technical school graduates to work in his "factory," the corner of a rented warehouse.

The immediate goal was to produce ceramic insulators for the TV makers. Since the need was acute and Inamori's quality standards were high, Kyocera made a profit from the start. Yet being a single-product company was not what Inamori had in mind. As he details in this book, he decided from the start that Kyocera would be a world-class company, a model for other ceramics makers everywhere. To this day he believes that this ambitious dream was the secret of Kyocera's consistent growth. "It was a basic part of our philosophy that we always wanted to do better," he says.

Doing better and getting bigger was more easily dreamed than done in Japan. The largest buyers of industrial ceramics all had their established suppliers: in a closed society, it was hard for an ambitious newcomer to break in. So Inamori decided to break out. He went to the United States.

In the early 1960s, several young American companies were just starting mass production of semiconductor chips, the basic commodity of the computer age. The chips required electrical insulators that would not block the flow of heat. Inamori told these firms that he could produce ceramic materials that would not conduct electricity but would conduct heat away from the chip. He then went back to Japan and spent months at the kilns, mixing various clays and chemicals to produce the insulators he had promised. By the end of the 1960s, Kyocera had become the world's biggest maker of semiconductor packages; in this essential commodity it still commands more than 65 percent of the global market today.

Many years later, Inamori recalled the challenges he faced when he decided to take his company into the semiconductor trade. His tiny start-up company was competing for contracts against some of the world's major ceramics giants, including Coors in the United States and Rosenthal in Germany. Inamori knew, he said, that Kyocera was no match for those firms in terms of facilities or investment. However, he also knew that none of the competitors would work any harder than he to get the mix just right, to adjust the kilns properly, and thus to produce the highest-quality product in the world.

To sit back and rest has no place in the Inamori philosophy, so Kyocera did not stand still once it had achieved dominance in semiconductor ceramic packages. The firm has moved into a broad range of new uses for applied ceramics: knives and scissors, musical instruments, jewelry, dental implants, hip joints, and so on. It is also one of the world's leading makers of solar cells.

As befits an industrialist who is constantly looking for the next challenge, Inamori has racked up some failures as well. Kyocera produced the world's first successful lap-top computer (the famous Radio Shack Model 100), but had to get out of the business as more established computer makers came charging along. Many investors doubted the wisdom of purchasing Yashica Camera Co., as it has long been a drain on Kyocera's earnings. "But," Inamori says today, "we were able to save the employees and finally make it into the only camera division that is profitable in Japan." Kyocera's Taito subsidiary, making portable karaoke machines, has yet to prove its worth.

However, Inamori's biggest venture outside the ceramics trade has turned into another runaway success. That was the decision, detailed in this book, to launch Japan's second long-distance telephone company. From that base, he moved into cellular telephone services, known as "Personal Handy Phone Systems," or "PHS," which have proven to be a smash success in Japan. In the process, the ceramics company is turning itself into a telecommunications company.

In Japan, Kazuo Inamori holds roughly the stature that Bill Gates enjoys in the United States. In fact, there is a good deal of similarity in the stories of these two men. Both bet early on a new technology, both devoted every ounce of their genius and strength to the task, and both built successful global corporations and huge personal fortunes.

The major difference—appropriate, perhaps, since Inamori is a generation older than Gates—is that Inamori has moved beyond the business world to become a sort of public philosopher of modern Japan. His views on Japan's traditional business community and stultified bureaucracy, which are set forth unflinchingly in this book, are now well known to his countrymen. So is his business philosophy—that is, the quasi-religious determination to support his employees and depend on them to produce the technology and the quality products required to succeed around the world.

In *For People—And for Profit*, Inamori sets out his people-centered philosophy of management. Although I don't think Inamori intended it this way, the book stands as a bold challenge to the lean-and-mean downsizing approach to management that is so strongly in vogue among Western corporations. In essence, Kazuo Inamori argues here that there is, in fact, another way—a more humane and less painful way—to achieve business success.

Kazuo Inamori writes Japanese that is very much in his own style—straightforward, clear, uncomplicated. That direct way of saying things was a godsend for a translator, and I am deeply grateful. I owe thanks as well to several others who helped with the task of rendering this book into English: Fumiaki Kuraishi, Shinkichi Kiuchi, Yasuko Maruta, Shigehiko Togo, and Akiko Kashiwagi. Homer Reid, an American college student whose Japanese skills are uncanny, played a major role. Finally, I'm grateful to Meagan Calogeras and Tetsuo Kuramochi at Kodansha International for asking me to produce the English edition of this important and timely book—and for their generous assistance along the way.

Tokyo, 1996   T. R. REID

MY VIEW OF JAPAN

The Japanese System: Back to Square One

The history of the human race in the twentieth century has been characterized by an ongoing revolution—the revolution in technology. Particularly in the years since World War II, the pace of change in new technology has been downright amazing, providing the crucial driving force in the world economy. In this way, the benefits of modern civilization have spread throughout the world.

Though many places in the world today have yet to receive the full thrust of this progress, the products of modern civilization—such as the growth of cities, new means of transportation and communication, cures for numerous diseases, increased average life expectancy, and significant improvements in living standards—have changed daily life to such an extent that for most people there is no comparison with the way things were just fifty years ago.

One other key impetus for this global growth was the development, under the United States' leadership, of a worldwide free market system. With the establishment of the simple free market principle—that economic activity should be allowed to cross international borders without restriction—the potential benefits for the human race have spread and blossomed.

Toward this end, nations have cooperated to lower tariffs and to unify the various systems for managing the world economy. The first major international agreement, the GATT (General Agreement on Tariffs and Trade), was designed to stimulate trade between nations, which was achieved with significant success. In late 1993, after a difficult series of negotiations known as the Uruguay Round, member nations reached agreement on a new framework, to be known as the World Trade Organization, or WTO. It is fair to say that this was another major step toward a worldwide free market system. This new structure will undoubtedly continue to stimulate the global economy as the basic market framework for the world.

Of all the nations that benefited from the free market system, postwar Japan emerged as one of the biggest winners. Japan's achievement has been called an "economic miracle," for the country rose quite literally from the ruins of war to its present position—as the world's second largest economy behind the United States. Today Japan has the highest per capita income in the world. Its cities are modern and functional; starvation and hunger no longer exist; and almost nobody lacks for clothing or shelter. Indeed, Japanese homes are filled with all kinds of electrical and electronic appliances, and more Japanese people than ever before are vacationing overseas. In short, Japan has become prosperous.

Much research has been done on the reasons behind this economic miracle. Personally, I feel it can be attributed to two main factors: the hard work of the Japanese people, and the worldwide free market system. Aided by these two assets, Japan has reached the highest pinnacle of economic maturity.

Faceless Japan

Today, however, Japan is frequently criticized by Western nations. There is increasing pressure from the United States with regard to Japan's trade surplus, and this confrontational attitude toward Japan is mounting steadily. Certainly, Japan's constant trade surplus has reached huge levels. However, this did not stem from unfair practices—unless, of course, it is considered unfair to work tirelessly to invest in and develop unproven foreign markets and to strive to provide customers with products of the highest quality. Japan has simply behaved in accordance with the principles of the free market.

Japan never set out to break the rules. Looking specifically at trade tensions with the United States, the fact remains that Japan used its industrial might to develop essentially independent systems of developing industries, from textiles to steel, automobiles, and machinery. Japan has given and continues to give as much consideration as possible to the United States while observing the principles of the free market. Yet complaints still persist that Japan is breaking the rules, that Japan is a unique force in the world.

Since the end of World War II, the Japanese have tried to turn their country into a peaceful, democratic nation and to contribute to the world through economic development. At least, that is how we see it. Yet angry accusations continue to surface intermittently, such as charges that Japan is aiming for world domination.

As a result, the Japanese feel that they are misunderstood—that criticism of this type stems from a failure to understand the mind of Japan. One example that is still fresh in my memory is our experience—a downright insulting one at that—in the 1990–91 Gulf War. Japan contributed the enormous sum of US$13 billion—the equivalent of US$100 for every Japanese citizen!—to the allied war effort; yet our contribution not only went unthanked but was also largely ignored by the international community.

Why did this happen?

Japan has the greatest industrial productive power in the world; our technological prowess, our research and development skills, and even our domestic market have grown to occupy significant positions in the world. The international community expects a nation of such awesome economic strength to act as befits a major nation. The fact that we are constantly criticized must mean that our actions as a nation are somehow flawed.

Certainly one problem that can be cited by critics is the overseas expansion of Japanese industries. By pouring massive quantities of products into foreign markets, an export surplus became inevitable. Sure enough, an enormous trade surplus began to accumulate, and the imbalance made Japan into a target of international criticism. However, the fact remains that Japanese products are of high quality, and it is only because foreign consumers demand them that Japan continues to make them, which results in a trade surplus. Thus, the Japanese people do not have the slightest idea why their companies should be criticized for producing good products that customers want to buy.

However, the fact is that Japan's industries employed a blitzkrieg strategy, exporting a veritable flood of products, targeted at specific markets, to boost their foreign market share. After years of cutthroat competition for domestic market share, the Japanese companies were ready to expand their efforts to the global market.

Japan has its own rationale for this type of behavior, which runs like this: after World War II, Japan was a small, defeated nation with no natural resources. Its only chance for survival lay in protecting its domestic industries and in trying to seize a slice of the foreign market pie. As a nation totally devastated by war, Japan had no choice but to be aggressive about defending its own interests.

This might have been acceptable back in the days when Japan was really a small nation, holding to its own culture in its own corner of the world. However, today that small, defeated nation has grown into one that controls 15 percent of the world's economy and has a per capita GNP to match that of the conquerors. The fundamental picture has changed. Japan now bears the responsibility of responding to global problems, and it must take world affairs into consideration when deciding its courses of action. This requires a completely new outlook.

Other countries complain that they cannot see the true face of Japan. If you think about it, that is not so surprising, since the Japanese themselves don't understand what their place in the present world should be. Other countries also criticize us for our impenetrable domestic markets. Isn't that because it is not only our markets but also our hearts that are closed to the world?

The *Mura* Theory: Village Society

I believe there is a historical reason for this situation. The Japanese race began its march toward civilization with wet-rice farming—that is, an agricultural system based on planting rice seedlings in a few inches of water inside enclosed paddies. This is an efficient way to produce large yields, but it also stamps societies that adopt it with a particular character. The overriding characteristic of wet-rice farming is that the collective decisions of the entire group are more important than the effort of a single individual.

Irrigation facilities are essential to paddy farmers. Constructing a system of causeways to secure a steady flow of water and distributing this fairly, without wastage, while moving it from high to low ground, is a considerable engineering feat. Furthermore, maintaining a system of water distribution—to arbitrate such decisions as where to lay runoff pipes in each water channel, which channels to dam and for how long, and how much water to allow each field—requires both an intricate system of rules and a strong authority to enforce them. It is not a system that any single person can manage by himself, no matter how hard he works. The system can only succeed if the entire village works together and agrees to abide by communal rules.

In addition, rice farming requires short-term, concentrated labor during the periods of planting and harvesting. Neglecting these can affect the size of the harvest itself. They are group operations that must be tackled in one fell swoop by the entire village working together. This is why, in the old days, a common labor organization called the *yui* was apparent everywhere in Japan. As a result of this, group activities became crucial. The corollary of this is that selfish behavior by any individual can cause severe damage to the crop, which is a matter of life and death for the group as a whole. The harvest is also heavily influenced by such climatic factors as rainfall, sunlight, and temperature. Overall, Japan's climate is warm and mild, making it suitable for rice farming.

On the other hand, take the example of nomadic societies, which were forced by severe environmental conditions to move around in search of material prosperity, a lifestyle that is conducive to raising livestock. In such a society, the fate of the group rests with the few leaders who control it. This tendency to depend on the abilities of a few individuals is entirely lacking in the Japanese. Rather, the Japanese put all their effort into the one, unmovable paddy, and after doing whatever is humanly possible, they leave the rest to nature. To them, the forces of the natural world apply uniformly to all. In this way, the concept of equality—that all individuals are fundamentally equal before nature—comes spontaneously to the Japanese.

In this kind of society, the best way to achieve abundance and prosperity is to work hard and cooperate honestly with one's neighbors and with nature. When your neighbor begins preparations for planting, you help. Imitating and utilizing the best methods will ensure an abundant harvest. In such a society, there is no need for individual talents. Imitation, rather than creativity, is the key to success.

The basic unit of rice farming is the community, or village—in Japanese the *mura*. The village is considered far more important than the individual. What is valued most of all is the commodity called *wa*, which is social harmony, or feeling of community. Getting along with the other members of the village is emphasized over individual concerns. Furthermore, it is essential that all members of the village be homogeneous and share this value system. Anybody who moves to the beat of a different drummer is considered a threat to the order of the village.

As long as each village—the basic unit of life—was able to maintain internal order, it continued to function. In contrast to a liberal system in which connections with the outside are emphasized, village society stresses the primary importance of the harmonious management of the community itself. People could not survive away from the village. People were bound to each other from birth, not by any sort of contract or plan, but by an inseparable bond of fate. To protect the internal order of the village, emotional bonds based on blood and land ties were valued and considered above logical arguments.

From another perspective, all this meant that if, for example, an inconsistency was discovered in the water distribution or any other system, an appropriate course of action could not be decided by logical discussion. This had the effect of making the situation tense and emotional. The accumulated tensions would smolder, for such problems were not able to be solved rationally.

Another problem arose when the village, which was accustomed to a harmonious, peaceful, and essentially equitable relationship among its members, had to deal with the outside world. There, community logic did not apply. When one community had to deal with another one, its actions could become highly contentious and competitive—at times, downright cruel. Actions that would never be tolerated against a member of the same community were allowed against a member of another community. In a sense, this was a double standard.

The principle of the village or community, which evolved together with wet-rice farming, survived until recent times. When Japan modernized along more Western lines during the Meiji era (1868–1912), the concept of freedom was imported. Yet even today the Japanese are not comfortable with and do not tolerate individualism easily. In other words, Japan has interpreted the concepts of freedom and the free market as free competition based not on the individual but on the group—the village.

It Is Time to Change Our Values

In 1868, at the start of the Meiji era, Japan began its shift to the modern era. Under the slogan "A Rich Nation, a Strong Army," Japan worked hard to catch up with the nations of the West. In the end, however, this build-up led to defeat by the Western alliance in a war of colonization. After the war, Japan abolished its large army and put all its efforts into economic development, rising from the ashes to build the world's second largest economy. Along the way there were a few transition points when, as a nation of the modern world, Japan was forced to change its views and its values. This seems to bear out what I call the "forty-year cycle theory" of modern Japanese history.

During the Meiji era, most Japanese dismissed pre-Meiji Japanese attitudes and methods as feudal and so abandoned them. Anything Western was praised and eagerly accepted. It is said that the wise men of the day really believed that they themselves had no history—they felt Japanese history began with the Meiji era. They dismissed the past and pushed ahead aggressively to strengthen the military, establish educational and financial systems, draw up a constitution, create a parliamentary system of government, build transportation and communication networks, and develop modern industries. The result was the first successful industrial revolution in Asia. Just forty years after emerging from isolation and feudalism, Japan went to war against Russia and defeated this key member of the Western alliance in the Russo-Japanese War (1904–5).

For an Asian country to defeat a Western one was an event of revolutionary proportions. You might say that Japan's heroic success shifted the locus of its dreams, so that catching up with the West was no longer its predominant ambition. However, the victory and Japan's emergence as a military power also gave cause for concern to many foreign countries. To be honest, it would have been much better if Japan had put the brakes on its "Rich Nation, Strong Army" policy right then.

Instead, Japan proceeded to annex Korea and moved at full speed to build a colonial empire. Denouncing foreign restrictions as unfair, Japan seceded from the League of Nations. It renounced the arms reduction limits of the Washington Naval Treaty of 1922 and set out on the road to isolation. There followed the invasion and occupation of mainland China, troop deployments to Southeast Asia, and eventually war with the United States. And, of course, the whole edifice came crashing down with the loss of several million Japanese lives, the bombing and ruin of all major Japanese cities, and the complete destruction of the country's productive capacity. Worst of all, Japan became the target of deep resentment because of its military occupation of neighboring Asian countries. Just forty years after its moment of triumph in the Russo-Japanese War, Japan suffered the humiliation of unconditional surrender.

This defeat, though, forced a transition. At long last Japan gave up military adventures; peace and economic development now became the national goals. Once again, the Japanese diligently set to work, and growth progressed to the point where Japan became the top global exporter. Now the nations of the world are complaining that Japan is occupying them once again—this time, economically.

An almost forty-year span separated the Meiji Restoration of 1868 and Japan's victory in the Russo-Japanese War; and exactly forty more years passed between that victory and

Japan's defeat in 1945. In essence, because Japan continued its course of the first forty years of hard work into the second forty years, the fruits of all that labor were wasted and the nation was left with nothing but massive debts.

Another forty years passed between the defeat in 1945 and the Plaza Accord of 1985—when the developing world's finance ministers, meeting at the Plaza Hotel in New York, agreed to fundamental reforms and increased the strength of the Japanese yen. In other words, at the same time that we were achieving unprecedented prosperity, we were also being harshly criticized by nations around the world.

Domestically, the economy grew and the yen was strong; yet there were serious questions as to whether the people of Japan achieved any real prosperity in their daily lives. Demands for reform of Japanese business methods arose both at home and abroad. The key question is whether we are about to repeat our sad past. If we press forward with current policies, if we refuse to slow down and rethink the social consensus that makes economic development our ultimate priority, will we not simply be repeating our prewar mistakes? Will we not once again be on the road to destroying our nation?

We have been pondering these issues for a decade now. During that time many suggestions have been made, including those for changes in our policies vis-à-vis the outside world and in the behavior of our industries, the search for zero-growth economic management, the reform of Japan's financial administration system, and government reform. The time has come for Japan, now an important citizen of the world, to be reborn.

The Meiji era reformers perceived that, in order for the nation to survive and flourish in the modern world, all aspects of the existing government, economy, and society had to be recreated from square one. And based on this concept, the Meiji leaders built a whole new country. However, succeeding leaders lacked the courage that sparked the first Meiji reformers.

They failed to respond to changes in the environment—and thus led the nation to ruin.

Our parents, the first postwar generation, have bestowed upon us our current prosperity, achieved through many successful reforms and with the guidance of the United States. And now, exactly five decades later, we are poised for another wave of major reforms. Our duty as second-generation postwar reformers, then, is clear. We need to rethink all aspects of the Japanese system—the structures built by our forefathers—and adapt them to the modern age. These may well have been the very systems that led Japan to prosperity after the war, and some of them, such as the bureaucracy, have greatly contributed to Japan's modernization in the more than one hundred years since the Meiji Restoration. Nonetheless, it is time for major changes. I feel we must learn from our Meiji forefathers. We must be prepared to tear down our institutions—our government, our administration, our education system, our system of industry, our economic management, everything—and rebuild them in the light of Japan's new position in the international arena.

And this does not only apply to our social institutions. In order to change the system, we must change our values. We must give up the paddy farmer value structure (of honoring the existing rules and preserving social harmony) and the village mentality of caring only about our own profit and maintaining order only in our own closed group. We must live as members of the world and contribute actively and aggressively, as an open nation, to the solution of global problems. If we fail in this essential task, we will face a real danger. The risk is that we will destroy ourselves—just as we did a few decades ago.

Chapter

2

Why Japanese Business Is Criticized Around the World

In the previous chapter I argued that Japan's postwar system must be completely reexamined and revamped. As a corporate man myself, I will give my view of current corporate practices and activities in Japan.

I have already noted that, as Japanese companies became huge exporters of goods to foreign countries, our trade surplus grew—and so did the backlash, in the form of criticism from around the world. Then, as Japanese companies started to introduce local production in various countries, Japanese factories, too, spanned the globe. These factories helped raise local employment levels, and by requiring a steady supply of parts, they also contributed to local industries. Since these products were shipped out to other countries—in many cases, back to Japan—these plants helped to increase the export figures of the countries where they were located. And since the factory workers took part in community work for schools and the like, the whole society could be seen to have benefited from this system.

Despite this, the attacks leveled against Japan have not slackened. We have even begun to see a trend toward regulations limiting the market share of all Japanese goods—not only those made in Japan but those produced in Japanese-owned factories abroad as well. Sadly, the success of these same factories has sometimes been a cause of international resentment.

When I visit the United States, I often refer to this problem in my speeches. I tell Americans that I would like them to remember their own immigrant traditions. I remind them that they are a people who have come together from the world over—that beneath their many different skin tones flows the blood of many nations. And aren't all these immigrant peoples treated equally under the U.S. Constitution? And isn't a foreign company doing business in the United States really just a "corporate immigrant"? Even if the capital or the technology comes from Japan, the company is operating under American laws. I'd like Americans to understand that these companies are making a contribution to American society by setting up their operations there.

Meanwhile, in Japan, a backlash is gaining momentum in response to these foreign criticisms. This argument runs as follows: Japanese companies are guilty of nothing but responding to demand. They have made and sold goods that customers want to buy. Since this is the basic principle of free trade, how can anybody criticize it? If making good products at good prices is considered wrong, then what is a company supposed to do? Japanese companies have worked extremely hard to stay at the forefront of technology, and American and European companies have been less diligent. Why, then, aren't they the targets of criticism?

This argument reflects the underlying feelings of Japanese corporate managers, but I don't agree with it. I don't think it is fair to say that the responsibility for what has happened belongs wholly to Western companies, or to say that they have let themselves lag behind in technological innovation and managerial skills. Who caused the problem? I think we have to admit that it is the Japanese companies which are to blame.

One prominent businessman has argued forcefully that "We should set higher prices for Japanese goods to account for their higher quality. That would soothe our foreign critics, and we could use the extra earnings to raise salaries and increase stockholders' dividends." However, I cannot agree with his suggestion, either. To produce abundant supplies of high-quality products at low prices is the basic objective of every industry. We cannot simply forsake the goal that every industry must always strive for.

The late Konosuke Matsushita—the founder of Matsushita Electric Industrial Co., Ltd., which is the world's biggest consumer electronics company and the parent of such brands as National and Panasonic—described his personal philosophy of business as "The Water Tap Philosophy." This basic principle of Matsushita Electric, he said, aimed at pouring out high-quality goods in abundance for the general public as reliably and steadily as water pours out of a faucet whenever people need it. To my mind, this concept remains valid today as the guiding principle for any industrial concern.

As for the criticisms from overseas, I don't think our foreign critics are accusing Japanese companies of ignoring the basic principles of free trade. Nor are they being criticized for their excellent technology, or because Western companies resent it when their domestic customers prefer Japanese-made products. I don't believe the criticisms stem from racial prejudice, either.

To me, the real reason behind such criticisms is not that Japanese companies are selling good products cheaply, but that they have rushed into foreign markets and unleashed—without the slightest concern for the fate of local producers—a veritable flood of products into those markets. These exporters have only one thought—their own profit. No matter how much they sell, they never say, "That's enough." Instead, they voraciously increase exports and grab so much market share that local producers cannot survive. That is the real problem.

The Result of Market-Share Mania

Why is it that Japanese companies always unleash such a flood of products into the market? The main reason is that they are terrified they will lose the market to a competitor if they don't sell as much as they can. Japan is an excessively competitive society, where you always stand to lose out to someone else if you don't seize your chances when you can.

A brief look at our postwar experience will help clarify this. As Japan set out to rebuild itself from a state of ruin, the people were living in extreme poverty. Consumer demand was weak at best, because consumers had no money to buy anything. In this sort of slim market, competition was bitter. And it was in these trying circumstances that the corporate stars of modern Japan—Matsushita, Sony, Honda, and the like—were born. At a time when the differences between products were very minor, the only way for a company to survive the competition was to increase market presence—that is, to beat out all the others for market share.

Later, as Japan's era of rapid growth began around 1960, the economy grew at a rate of 10 percent or so every year. Japanese companies expanded at a furious pace and moved to large-scale mass production. However, it was still only in the struggle for ever-greater market share that the business world found any sense of security. In this sort of competition, corporations became obsessed with their ranking in each market, which was measured by market share. Thus, even as a general sense of order emerged in the various industries, there was still heated competition to take market share away from others. Beyond this competition, companies also competed in investments in new facilities. This drive for increasing investment in productive capacity accounts for much of the dynamism of Japan's postwar economy.

While protecting the domestic market against imports from foreign firms, Japanese companies rode the wave of the international free trade system created by GATT and suchlike, and commenced expanding overseas in a major way. Just as they had done in the domestic market, Japanese firms set out to attain a significant market share around the world. Having advanced into foreign countries and achieved a sizable share of the market there, they were able to cut prices. Since they were thus able to turn out large quantities of goods at prices their competitors couldn't match, these companies prevailed in global competition. Within fifty years of Japan's defeat and destruction in World War II, its companies—through constant efforts to improve production and increase market share— were winning the struggle for market share all over the world. Who could have predicted this state of affairs? Who, seeing the shattered state of postwar Japan, would have believed that the same country would reach the point where it is today, with Japanese companies occupying the top ranks among the world's leading business concerns?

Japan's Self-righteous Companies

This system of putting market share first functioned almost faultlessly as long as the domestic and export markets were growing. With regularly expanding markets, there was steady new investment in plant and equipment, which pushed up market share even higher. This business strategy, aimed at long-range profit rather than immediate returns, was the core principle of what came to be known, and respected, around the world as "Japanese-style management."

However, it was also a fact that many major firms in other countries lost their market share in the face of this Japanese onslaught. In both the United States and Europe, companies headed down a bitter path, from layoffs to factory closures to bankruptcy. As workers in these countries lost their jobs, criticisms of Japanese companies increased. These firms' ceaseless pursuit of market share, their sweeping advance into more and more foreign markets, and their flood of exports made them dominant in global markets. As this ferocious competitive style continued, and as the flood of Japanese exports and Japanese production capacity grew, attacks against Japan began to grow as well.

What has brought us to this situation? One reason may lie in the Japanese perception of "freedom," which is substantially different from the Western view of that concept. In the nineteenth-century business world, when Japan first entered the global marketplace, the principles of classical liberalism ruled—which might be regarded as a case of the strong devouring the weak. This world view is reflected in the Japanese understanding of the word "freedom," which is often taken to mean something close to "the freedom to do whatever you want." As I said earlier, the Japanese people have accepted the free market economy as a guarantor of free collective capitalism. And yet we still harbor a deep-rooted fear about whether Japan's group culture, and the individuals within the group, can survive the rigors of truly free competition.

The cultural history of Japan, centered on the principle of the group, as discussed in Chapter 1, is clearly mirrored in the activities of the modern Japanese corporation. In Japan, competition in a free market is often compared to a world where the law of the jungle reigns: "Only the strong survive"—that sort of thing. However, in the natural world it is plain that there is perfect order, and even the strongest of animals live in accordance with that order. Lions and other carnivores only kill their prey for food. Once these big beasts have eaten their fill, even the weakest animals can approach them without risk, because, once sated, they will not hunt and kill again. Given enough food to sustain life, they have no reason to. Carnivorous animals seem to realize that if all their prey were wiped out, their own existence would be threatened, and they know instinctively how to live in synergy with smaller animals. I believe that tribes of humans that live by hunting possess the same innate reasoning and knowledge.

In this way, the Western ideal of freedom does not equal

"Do whatever you want." In the era of nineteenth-century liberalism, the key concept in Western Europe, and an important precursor of capitalism, was the "Protestant ethic." Its basic principle was that men should work hard—that was God's will. They should produce as much as possible and use the fruits of their labor to serve the principle of "Love thy neighbor." By the same token, it was important to eliminate waste and use resources wisely. And from this moral standard grew the practice of accumulating capital and using it to create new enterprises. This was the birth of capitalism.

The people who invented capitalism never forgot their responsibility to honor God. This meant they could earn a decent profit (but should avoid profiteering), and they also felt obliged to provide some benefit, some contribution, to society as a whole. Thus, Western societies are based on the principle of individual liberty. Although on a superficial level this may look little different from the law of the jungle, at a deeper level it is a way of life that is firmly rooted in the principle of self-control. And from this follows the basic social rule that you may consume no more than you need to live—that you must not waste resources.

On the one hand, this might be deemed the influence of Christianity. On the other hand, it could be the heritage of people's hunter-gatherer ancestors, who always took care to give their prey a chance to reproduce. Or it could even be a result of the maturation of society. Whatever the underlying causes, despite occasional periods of tyranny, Western society has generally followed a set of social rules based on this inborn principle of self-control.

From this perspective, we can readily understand why Japanese companies are perceived to be breaking the rules. Unaware of the principle of self-control, at a certain point in their history they stumbled upon a distorted understanding of the word "liberalism" and acted self-righteously on that misunderstanding. This was not tolerable, for in the world of

Western companies—the companies that created and operated in the Western market—to strip the field clean strictly for your own gain is not permissible.

Learning from Traditional Market Law

Kyocera was founded in the city of Kyoto, the ancient capital of Japan and home to many business operations that carry on customs dating back several centuries. A traditional commercial law still operates there, and it offers some important lessons for modern times.

At one famous pickled vegetable store, only two barrels of pickles are put out for sale each day. In the morning, before the store opens, customers line up outside the door. And when that day's allotment has been sold, the store closes. Even if there are more customers waiting to buy, the store still shuts its doors, putting up a notice saying, "Those who want to buy, please do us the honor of coming back tomorrow." The reason is that the flavor of the pickles starts to decline almost immediately after they are at their best, and since the shop prefers to deal only in products of the highest quality, it controls production to maintain its standards.

Here we see that familiar principle at work again: neither buy nor sell more than what is necessary. If the day's allotment is sold out by noon, that gives the proprietors more time to start preparing the next day's batch. Then at night they can go out to the theater or enjoy some other form of recreation. In this way they use their free time to support the cultural life of the city. Of course, there are many pickle stores, each with its own special recipe, and because every one offers a unique flavor of pickles, they can all stay in business. The point here is that they do not compete on price or quantity but on quality— how good the pickles are. It is competition based, if you will, on the individual character of each merchant's product. Through differences in the character of the product, each store creates its own market. It is the mercantile version of "live and let live," a philosophy of "sell and let sell." Each store produces a set quantity of pickles at a reasonable cost, and there's enough business for all to survive.

For other traditional businesses in Kyoto, such as those of Japanese-style cakes and the famous Kiyomizu pottery, the pattern followed is similar. In order to preserve the essential hand-crafted quality, you can only produce a limited quantity. There are countless old shops like this in Kyoto, busily producing their unique products for a limited clientele. Relying on their individuality, maintaining a small but steady trade, they are preserving the traditional style of commerce in Kyoto. These merchants take care not to invade one another's turf—and they, in turn, can feel safe from invasion themselves.

During Japan's feudal Edo era (1603–1868), a famous Kyoto Confucian and ethics philosopher named Ishida Baigan (1685–1744) taught that "The true merchant thinks first of the customer's position, and then of his own." Baigan's philosophy was called "Shingaku," or "Heart Learning." As the name suggests, it centers on understanding the workings of the human heart and the human spirit. Through self-control in accordance with the human spirit, Baigan taught, man can achieve happiness. Until quite recently, courses in Shingaku were still being offered in downtown Kyoto.

One key difference between the traditional Kyoto rules of business and the practices of modern corporations involves the basic issue of creativity versus discipline. In my view, the Japanese corporation's penchant for excessive competition, for market-share-at-any-cost, rests on what I will call the "Imitation Principle." This implies that as soon as one company develops a new idea and makes it successful, all the other firms immediately jump in and start producing imitations. Since the successful model has just been launched, the latecomers can concentrate their efforts on cutting costs and making it cheaper. It is a relatively simple thing to sell basically the same product at a lower price than the pioneer in the field.

Thus, competitors invade the market—a market created by the original producer—and start vying for market share. This is competition based on identical products.

The pioneering firms know full well that if they just sit back and take it easy, they will lose their market to the new entrants. So from the beginning they aim to maximize market share, forcing up production to prepare for rigorous competition. As the pioneer and the imitators step up the competition, production capacity frequently outstrips demand. Then the Japanese firms send the excess products overseas, in an export drive that causes chaos in foreign markets.

It is true, of course, that the Imitation Principle proved extraordinarily useful to Japan in the past century or so, as the country eagerly embraced all foreign ideas and foreign technology in its drive for modernization. And it is equally true that the success of many Japanese companies did not derive entirely from direct imitation. Many of them have also adapted basic research from the West to produce better and cheaper products. However, the time when we can prosper through the Imitation Principle has come to an end, and Japan must refrain from the tendency to jump into markets and compete with copycat products. It is essential to exercise self-restraint and stop invading markets created by innovative companies. Only in this way can we avoid the bitter resentment of corporations whose goods we copy.

Even if Japanese industry stopped competing with identical goods, there would be no need to worry that Japan's standard of living would fall. On the contrary, it would be a great boon if there was more competition in creativity, if Japanese companies were racing one another to get innovative new products on the market. What's more, the opening of such new markets could revive Japan's economy.

Copycat production, it must be said, is a low-risk enterprise. It is a way to increase the efficacy of invested capital. In contrast, when it comes to creating innovative designs and forging new markets for such products, a lot of risk is involved, but this is the essence of the new type of management we need: to develop technological innovations and new ideas, and to spur new demand for new products.

As I will point out in Part 2 of this book, if Japan's corporate giants are to be welcomed in the industrial world, Japan will have to build a society based on fair competition. That will require self-regulation and a conscious decision to act with restraint. Both at home and abroad, Japanese companies have to hold to a course of fairness and move step by step to act with responsibility.

Why Creativity Isn't Valued

If we seek to understand why the Imitation Principle is so firmly established in Japan, we will find the answer in the tradition of wet-rice paddy farming, the agricultural system of most East Asian societies. In the realities of existence with this method of cultivation lies the basis of Japan's aversion to creativity, for in wet-rice cultures the work and knowledge or wisdom of the group had to come first.

The Imitation Principle can be seen in another, more modern manifestation as well. In Japan's rush to modernize in the Meiji era, a great influx of modern ideas and products came from overseas. The most up-to-date and the most fashionable goods were foreign-made. This imported culture was an explosive success. Demand for these modern items was extremely strong—but prices were also extremely high. To create more affordable prices for these much-desired goods, Japanese manufacturers began copying them and manufacturing them to meet soaring domestic demand.

Even today, when Japanese companies have become major players in markets around the world, the notion that imports are somehow better still carries weight among the Japanese people. For example, in the fields of medicine and pharmaceuticals, it is conventionally accepted in Japan that American and

European products are best. This attitude has had an important impact on Japan's standards for assessing good technology. I learned this firsthand in the late 1950s, just before Japan embarked on its period of rapid growth.

In those days, the Japanese held the view that the best engineer was the one who could turn out a decent replica of any new Western product within a year after news of the innovation first reached Japan. An engineer who could copy a product after reading a description in a catalogue was rated next best. Someone who could make a copy only after obtaining the actual item was considered a third-rate engineer. And anybody who couldn't copy a Western product was written off and relegated to the lowest rung of the engineering ladder. Yet a Japanese engineer with a creative idea that had not yet been developed in the West was considered even lower, as useless. No attention was paid to any new idea unless it had gained acceptance in the West. Since the highest esteem went to those who could copy Western engineering, no effort was spent on being creative. To some extent, this attitude survives to this day

As a matter of course, no Japanese banks would finance projects based on Japanese technology. However, investments for technology imported from the West were quickly approved. Another contributing factor was the government's restrictive stance, even after wartime controls had been abolished. In the postwar period, "administrative guidance" from the government essentially determined which companies would get capital investment and which companies would get permits to import technology from abroad. And the government, of course, favored companies that toed the line. A company that was determined not to embark on any innovations at all was considered a good company. This attitude persisted long after the war—strict government regulation and guidance in many major industries meant that when new technology was introduced, it was done under the auspices of governmental regulation and approval. Industrial "combines," which were formed in accordance with the bureaucrats' overall plans, were commonplace.

In this system, it was generally believed that, rather than risk trying something new, it was more advantageous to the nation to restrict creative urges from within the company and stick to the path of imitation.

Management That Stresses Personality

The criticism that Japan's industrial giants gained their present position in world markets by copying Western technology is still prevalent. While not 100 percent accurate, it is generally correct—and I'm not the only person who would say so. Moreover, the Imitation Principle has held sway not only in technology but also in Japanese society and consumer habits.

Many "new companies" created after the war were basically copies of American models. Some perspicacious managers, recognizing the obvious—that anything successful in the United States would eventually succeed in Japan—set off to pay homage to the United States and learn what was happening there.

As Japan gradually came level with the leading nations of the world, we began to see the reverse: products going from Japan to markets around the world. In technology and human resources, Japan ranked with the best. And yet, even as its companies pulled themselves up to a position of equality with the world's industrial leaders, Japan, the "copycat country," still drew condescending smiles on the world stage. Even if it were true that Japanese enterprises had lacked creativity, this was not due to the lack of creativity on the part of individual Japanese people.

When a foreign company launches a new product, it is manifesting a strong determination to try something innovative, which stems, in turn, from an atmosphere where creativity is considered a plus. That is why Japanese companies must abandon a corporate culture that reflects a determination only to try things that others have already done. For this, it is essential to recognize the importance of basic research, to design a corporate system that fosters creative ideas, and to educate employees in this approach.

Today, companies can gather both talented people and research results from all over the world, and even in Japan many bright, highly individualistic people can be found. Yet in order to employ people with creative personalities fruitfully, companies need a culture that supports and promotes the spirit of creativity. To do that, it is essential to stay at the leading edge of innovative research.

To encourage creativity and a management style that takes into account individual personalities, Japanese companies need to rethink their peculiar employment system and the habit of putting the corporation first. Instead of focusing on what is good for the whole organization, we must instill a system that emphasizes the merits of the individual. This is also, by the way, something that's necessary to create a genuine democracy, or a society based on what is best for each person. At the same time, in place of economic management centered on the select few, we need to change to an economy that concerns itself with the masses, the ordinary consumers. Unfortunately, I recognize that encouraging creativity is not something that can be done overnight.

When Kyocera was first established thirty-five years ago in Kyoto, it was a tiny operation with only twenty-eight employees. Since bigger, more established firms could attract all the human resources and investment capital they wanted, it was obvious that Kyocera wouldn't get anywhere if it just tried to compete with copycat products, so it had no choice: from the moment of its inception, Kyocera was managed on the idea of "innovate or bust."

Since we couldn't survive by imitating others, we had to do what nobody else was doing. Kyocera would chart virgin territory. We encouraged creativity; we nurtured personality;

we set out from the first with the dream of achieving world leadership in ceramics. And I firmly believe it was because we had that dream that Kyocera became the company it is today.

For Japan to encourage creativity, though, it is not enough for individual corporations to concentrate on it. The whole nation needs to support it. Society has to emphasize individuality and promote creative thinking, which places a crucial burden on the education system.

I think it is doubtful that Japan will ever succeed in encouraging creativity and individualism. After all, by definition, a creative new idea is one that defies conventional wisdom, and such an idea is apt to be criticized at first. The fact is you can't make any creative proposal unless you're willing to take the heat in the form of attacks from conventional thinkers. To be able to bear such onslaughts requires a strong personality, and to create a population of strong individuals requires a climate of tolerance in the society as a whole.

Japanese society is permeated with such traditional sayings as "The nail that sticks up gets hammered down," and "If you can't beat 'em, join 'em." The harmony of the group has always had a higher priority than the interests of any single member, so the person who thinks differently from others is treated as an outcast. In this kind of society, creative ideas tend to get nipped in the bud.

In Japan's educational system, too, everybody is expected to walk in step with everybody else, whether in the classroom or in daily life. This rule is intended to maintain social order, since those who can't fit in are routinely cast aside. It's not unexpected that some children dislike school, for individual tastes and personalities vary even among children. It is normal for kids to differ on their favorite foods, their favorite subjects, and so on. However, in Japan's school system, students are all treated like identical seeds that are expected to sprout and blossom in exactly the same way. With the goal of passing the entrance exam for a top-ranking school, they are trained parrot-fashion to give automatically the right answers to exam questions. Selecting a school is equally automatic. The school's atmosphere and curriculum are secondary concerns; parents are expected to choose the school that is most prestigious in society's eyes. And by the time these students enter college, they are completely lacking in any individuality.

Recently, it has been said that values are become more varied in Japan's society and that there is more tolerance for individual thinking. However, in daily life, and even in the family, the person who sets forth a dissenting view is generally ignored and accorded little attention or respect—as if he were out of line with standard values. The person who makes his own choice or who adopts a lifestyle different from everybody else's may be accepted in his own circle, but he will not be accepted by society as a whole. Similarly, both private companies and the government tend to shun ideas that have not been tried out before. Rather than acting on a new idea, they will sit back and proceed cautiously, and only move in the accepted way.

In summary, the tendency to stick to precedent and preserve the established order, with all companies proceeding at the same pace, still dominates in Japan. It will be a long time before it develops a culture that really values creativity. If Japan genuinely hopes to stimulate creativity, it will have to break with custom and recognize the importance of ideas that challenge conventional wisdom. It needs to learn to value the unconventional, to tolerate uncommon opinions and untried ways of looking at familiar things. For Japan, a society that treasures conformity and adherence to precedent, encouraging creativity will require a massive shift in both Japan's social conventions and its educational system.

Chapter 3

Living in a Global Society

According to Takeshi Umehara, a professor at the International Research Center for Japanese Studies, in the Jomon period (ca. 10,000–300 B.C.), when the people led a hunting and gathering style of life, the Japanese lived in harmony with nature. Excavation of remains from that period provide valuable insights into the lifestyle of the people then, and seeds, animal bones, and seashells have been found. Among more recent discoveries are rice husks and traces of paddy fields. The Jomon people, it seems, had learned how to cultivate rice.

Interestingly, however, among excavated remains of the subsequent archeological Yayoi period (ca. 300 B.C.–A.D. 300)—when rice farming became prevalent—were found skulls with holes in them and backbones with embedded arrowheads. These are not found in remains from Jomon times, which indicates that warfare occurred in the Yayoi period.

In this way, although our image of hunters and gatherers is generally one of savages, excavations from that period reveal no indications of battles or massacres. On the other hand, while the image of an agricultural people is one of peaceful village life, it is among the remains of this period that we have found the first evidence of warfare.

Professor Umehara explains that this is because the spread of farming brought with it the beginning of food storage. In rice-farming societies, the entire year's supply of this basic staple is gathered at harvest time, and it has to be stored. Though rice farming made food plentiful and life stable, storing rice was essential to prepare for future eventualities. When word got out that some village had large stores of rice, the village would be attacked and the stores of grain stolen. The history of warfare and plundering begins with greed.

The Philosophy of Circulation and Regeneration

In Jomon times, people lived surrounded by abundant forests. Their hunting and gathering style of life was blessed with food from the mountains, such as fruits, nuts, and animals, and also with food from the sea, such as fish, seaweed, and shellfish. They are said to have lived in accordance with the natural cycle, gratefully accepting nature's gifts and praying for similar blessings in the future. There was none of the disruption of nature that was characteristic of later, so-called civilized periods. These people had the wisdom to take only what they needed from nature, and did not interfere with nature's powers of regeneration.

Professor Umehara compares the lifestyle of this period with the festival of Iyomante of the Ainu (an indigenous tribe of Hokkaido, northern Japan). The festival is held after a successful bear hunt to send the bear's soul into the next world. The Ainu pray that the soul thus freed will become a bear again and return to their land, providing them once more with delicious meat and useful skin and fur.

This is the philosophy behind the cycle of regeneration in the forest. If everybody decided to capture more bears, the animal would be unable to reproduce and soon would become extinct. Then the people would lose the foundation of their lives. If nature does not regenerate, people who live off nature's bounty must either change their lifestyle or, in extreme cases, die of starvation.

The Jomon people, living in accordance with the natural cycle and dependent on its gifts for survival, seem to have understood that disrupting nature meant eventual destruction of themselves. With the advent of livestock farming and agriculture, we see the beginnings of man's attempt to control nature. Civilization imposed man-made methods on nature, in proportion to the increase of greed, and soon the natural cycle was destroyed. Waves of prosperity alternated with troughs of poverty—a pattern that is repeated over and over again. Particularly with the modern industrial civilization that began in Europe, men devoted themselves to developing tools to conquer nature and create a richer materialistic lifestyle. However, the corollary was that the environment and the global regeneration mechanism, on which mankind's very existence depends, began to suffer critical damage.

Today, as threats to our global environment are being denounced, should we not, as the people who created these threats in the name of civilization, learn from the wisdom of the hunters and gatherers of the Jomon period? We should learn from their philosophy that living things coexist as part of nature's cycle of regeneration. In other words, it is time to halt the unrestrained progress of our modern civilization.

I like to call this the "philosophy of coexistence and regeneration"; or, in honor of our Jomon ancestors who shared the resources of the forest with its other inhabitants, the "forest philosophy."

The Wisdom of African Hunters

Junichiro Itani, professor emeritus of Kyoto University and one of the world's leading authority on primates, has carried out research on the communities of wild chimpanzees living in the mountains of Congo and on native African communities which exist in harmony with nature. It was from him that I heard the following story.

One day, on his way to visit the mountain where the chimpanzees lived, he passed through a small village, so he had a chance to observe the way the people there hunt. All the men in the village set off together, but as soon as someone kills a large animal such as a deer or zebra, the hunt is over for the day. The entire group stops and carries the catch back to the village, led triumphantly by the hunter who made the kill.

On reaching the village, this hunter skins the animal in front of his house. The entire village gathers to watch, and then everybody helps to divide the meat up, following their own rules about what part, and what quantity, the family of the man responsible for the kill may take. After this, the amount given to each family depends on the closeness of their blood ties to the hunter's family.

Interestingly, after each family receives its share, there is a further division among relatives—again according to the closeness of the blood relationship. The more distant a relative, the smaller his or her share. Once a person receives his share, he further divides it and gives some away. The result is that each person in the village receives more or less the same amount. Professor Itani was deeply impressed by how food is distributed in this way throughout the village. Although we think of such tribes as being primitive or uncivilized, they maintain a definite orderly and fair system and have arrived at an excellent way to guarantee equitable distribution. Itani wondered if any villagers had the desire for more and asked one of them, "Why don't you go kill another animal?" "No, I couldn't do that," was the man's prompt reply.

Especially noteworthy is the fact that this forest "philosophy of coexistence and regeneration" is observed not only by human beings but even by primates. According to Itani, chimpanzee societies exhibit similar behavior. Chimpanzees are omnivores, and although their diet consists mainly of fruit and leaves, they also eat meat. In fact, chimpanzees are extremely strong animals, and they occasionally hunt deer and other large animals. In this case, the chimpanzees also hunt as a group, but, here again, as soon as a large animal is killed, they all stop and gather around the successful hunter, who then tears off a share of meat for each of the others.

Professor Itani says, "At first I thought this distribution system was primitive societal behavior, seen only in primates and 'uncivilized' communities. But then I realized that it was simply the wisdom of suppressing one's greed and coexisting with nature."

It is a manifestation of the same wisdom that we see in the Jomon people's concepts of coexistence and regeneration. Even primates such as chimpanzees and undeveloped communities suppress their greed in order to coexist with nature.

Slash-and-Burn Farming

Near the forest where the chimpanzees live is a small village of slash-and-burn farmers. In this style of farming, a section of forest is cut down, burned, and the soil that is enriched with the ash is planted with crops. These farmers are friendly people, and they treated Professor Itani and his party hospitably whenever they visited. On one such occasion, the village elder said to him, "Last year, after you left, some people from another area came, and after that we didn't have enough food for ourselves." It seemed that although the village only produced as much food as it needed for one year, the villagers were giving much of that away to visitors.

Since this obviously resulted in a food shortage, Itani asked why the village didn't foresee the arrival of guests and produce more food? "Actually," replied the elder, "the gods wouldn't allow it." Apparently such food shortages caused by the arrival of visitors occur every year.

Using primitive farming implements, the natives carry out their slash-and-burn farming in an area of forest within walking distance of their village. Since they don't use any fertilizer, after a few years of farming the soil becomes barren and no crops will grow. When this happens, the villagers move to another section of forest and cut it down and burn it, so the process is repeated. Assuming the forest surrounding their village is divided into ten sectors, and the natives move every six years, they will return to the original area in sixty years. By that time, the trees and plant life will have grown back, and the entire process can be repeated. Slash-and-burn farming involves burning the forest and thus might appear harmful to the environment, but, in fact, when carried out in accordance with the natural cycle, it is an excellent regenerative system. The slash-and-burn farmers have totally mastered the technique of coexisting with the forest.

However, if the villagers increase their consumption and expand the area under cultivation, the length of the cycle will be shortened and the forest will be burned before it has completely recovered. The soil will not be sufficiently enriched, so obtaining the same yield will necessitate extending the area under cultivation. However, this will automatically shorten the span of the cycle further, until eventually the cycle will be broken. The destruction of the forests will continue, but slash-and-burn farming will no longer be possible. All that will remain will be barren earth.

The notions of coexistence and cyclic regeneration prevalent in pre-civilized societies have much to teach us about our own economic activities, for when these disrupt the natural cycle, and metaphorically strip the entire forest of its regenerative capacity, they will eventually jeopardize the very foundation our existence as humans beings is built upon.

Coexistence and the Regenerative Cycle

In animal and plant societies, different types of organisms adapt to their habitats and the food they eat, finding appropriate environments for themselves in order to "coexist." In human societies as well, while recognizing that we are all different, we coexist to allow mutual development. This is the essence of life on the earth.

A few years ago, "coexistence" became something of a trendy word. First, Japan's Keidanren (Federation of Economic Organizations), a body of powerful business leaders, began using it, followed by financial circles and the bureaucracy, and eventually its use spread throughout society. Actually, there is also the biological word "symbiosis," which refers to two different species living together in a way that benefits both. In business terms, this might seem similar to an exclusive industrial group relationship or "collusion," and for this reason some economists assert that "coexistence" is simply an approving euphemism for cartels.

I think of coexistence as simply meaning "living together," as distinct from symbiosis. It describes the ideal of all organisms on earth existing with a basic mutual respect for one another, and this involves suppressing one's individual desires. All life on earth depends upon living together, and behind this lies the principle of the life cycle, that living things all support one another in some way.

Even predators, which must kill a certain quantity of prey in order to live, instinctively know that if they kill more, their prey will become scarce—jeopardizing the existence of the predators themselves. Acting solely for one's immediate benefit ultimately threatens the basis of one's own existence. Human beings, like any other animal, have no way of escaping this.

Therefore, to fulfill the ideal of living together, it is necessary to be aware of the principles of regeneration, to control our boundless greed, and to live with restraint. Without self-control, coexistence is not possible.

Living Together in Society
As our civilization has prospered, our individual desires have grown to such massive proportions that we must take heed of

the Buddhist exhortation, "Be content with what you have!"

Not a few managers have made their companies profitable and built up a good reputation, only to end up making mistakes that bankrupt their companies. When someone is successful, he is spoiled by people around him. As he rises higher, he is treated better and better. His success may be a result of his cautious and correct decision-making, but he may forget all that and grow overconfident. Enveloped by a luxurious lifestyle and absorbed in his selfish interests, he may eventually act against common sense and attempt something impracticable and impossible. People around him will whisper, "In the old days, when the company was just starting, he wasn't like this. He used to be so reliable." The more successful such a person becomes, the more he risks losing people's support. Treading a path to disaster, he is the perfect example of someone who doesn't understand "Be content with what you have!"

It's surprising how many managers of small and medium-sized companies think the company belongs to them alone. There might even be a few such managers in large corporations. As soon as you start to think, "This company is mine—it exists for me; as long as I'm making a profit, all is well," your ego becomes inflated, you begin to make decisions based only on what suits you, and you will inevitably make mistaken decisions that will cause damage to the company you worked so hard to build.

A company might be likened to a small forest. The managers have to think about how best to live with the employees, who live in the forest. If your employees do not prosper, then you cannot prosper. The key point for the manager is to make everybody, both management and employees, happy, and if they are all happy, the small forest, or the company, will prosper.

To continue with this metaphor, society is a larger forest surrounding the company. There are investors, who provide capital; suppliers, who provide parts and materials; and customers, who buy the products. If any of these elements is missing, no company can be successful. Society represents a kind of cycle, and it is the basis of the existence of industry. In the natural rhythm of this forest, with profits circulating among its constituents—employees, investors, suppliers, and consumers —the conditions for the continuance of the cycle of industry are maintained.

Within society, companies must coexist in competition. Managers must be aware of the principles of this cycle and make the company function as a part of it. They must develop the wisdom to live together in this economic cycle.

Philanthropy and a Respect for a Plurality of Values

Society has developed and progressed by allowing and tolerating a plurality of values. In Japan after the Meiji era, however, a balance between these differing values was lost. The nation became the highest priority, and strengthening it by building up the military was emphasized above all else. In the same way, the last half-century has seen a similar imbalance. We may have abandoned military strength, but we now place an equally strong emphasis on economic values: all undertakings have been more or less ranked according to their contribution to the economy.

Companies naturally operate with economic strength as their objective, but at the same time it is essential to respect the plurality of human and cultural values and to strike a balance between these and economic values. Fortunately, however, as Japanese society has matured, the importance of cultural, rather than merely economic, values has recently begun to be addressed.

One example of this can be seen when companies support cultural and social activities such as the arts or scientific research through philanthropy. Another example is the recent tendency for company employees to take part in community activities. These are both important and necessary for a company seeking to coexist with society at large. Of course, such activities are only possible when the company is making a profit, but it is admirable indeed for a company to return part of its profit to society in its scope of operation, and to make an effort to help the world and its inhabitants in general.

This trend is not limited to companies, either. Using one's individual talents, time, or resources to help society not only brings joy to the giver but is highly meaningful to society. It should be commended. Similarly, it is important for a company to support its workers' volunteer activities. In Western Europe, perhaps because of its Christian background and tradition, this kind of activity has long been an essential element of society, and individual initiatives in this respect are highly regarded and encouraged.

Japan has had a similar tradition at various times in its history, but current Japanese institutions—laws, employment practices, pensions, and taxes—are still sadly wanting with regard to stimulating social activity by either individuals or companies. In particular, in the current tax code, charitable donations are not tax-deductible.

Since the dawn of Japan's modern era about 120 years ago, the country has failed to recognize the importance of volunteer activities on the part of both individuals and companies, and has failed to develop an environment to stimulate them. It seems almost as though, at some point in the course of modern history, a division of labor was agreed on: the government would assume all socially necessary tasks, while individuals and businesses would look out for themselves—quite the opposite of the Western tradition of supporting charitable causes. Over time, this attitude has hardened into a rule. Individuals and private businesses have come to feel that the good of the general public lies outside their mission, so they have concentrated solely on their profits. This was mistaken, of course—and it has been costly both for business and for society.

Such a cold and aloof corporate stance will undoubtedly

prove unacceptable on the international stage, too. Now that Japan, the Japanese people, and Japanese companies have come to occupy a central role in the world, we must face up to the question of what we can do to solve common problems in the areas of peace, human rights, poverty, and the environment. Japanese companies have much to do before the Japanese people can become respected citizens of the world.

It is clear that in promoting creative efforts such as cultural activities and scientific research in order to realize human potential, the initiative of individuals should be encouraged rather than all relevant decisions being entrusted to the government. Ideally, corporate social activities such as cultural philanthropy should be based the activities of individual citizens in a wide range of fields, and should complement those activities to bring them to fruition. Corporate activities will find their true function when they help to stimulate the activities of individual citizens.

Coexistence in a Global Society

The desire to lead a life that is even slightly more comfortable and luxurious has been the driving force behind the progress of modern society. Today's material wealth is a result of this selfish human desire. However, our affluent civilization has now reached its limits, and is threatening our very existence by causing environmental problems across the globe.

To avoid disaster, it is necessary for us to learn from the wisdom of our ancestors. As I mentioned before, this includes understanding the principle of natural regeneration, controlling the greed that has provided the stimulus for civilization's progress, restricting the insatiable expansion of economic activities, and learning to coexist with other living things.

Corporate projects such as the support of cultural activities and Keidanren's One Percent Club—in which Japanese firms voluntarily commit themselves to spend one percent of their earnings on philanthropic endeavors—are evidence that greed is being brought under control. These activities serve to counterbalance the pervading obsession with self-interest and, through them, Japan's corporate world may become more humane and may eventually come to gain the respect of people around the world.

The process of controlling our selfish desires and ambitions naturally inspires a greater concern for others. By being less selfish, by learning from our mistakes, by being humble, and by learning to be satisfied, we foster a spirit of caring for our fellow human beings.

Looking at things with a self-centered attitude makes it impossible to see beyond what lies immediately before us. Conversely, adopting an attitude of concern for others naturally broadens one's horizons and helps one see the true value of things. As this spirit grows in one's heart, the entire forest comes into view: one begins to see the entire planet as being in a state of coexistence.

It is a fact that Japan's economy cannot grow forever. It is neither possible, nor permissible, for the economies of the advanced nations, including Japan's, to continue growing while the problems of less fortunate nations are ignored. Japan must try to restrict the growth of its gigantic economy. It has often been noted that the advanced nations account for only 20 percent of the world's population but consume 80 percent of the world's resources. If the advanced nations aim for further growth, they will consume even more resources. If they continue their consumption of world resources at this rate, what is left for developing nations will decrease proportionately.

In order to control rocketing birth rates and bring standards of living closer to those of the advanced nations, developing nations must increase their industrialization—a necessary step that will automatically increase their consumption of resources. Thus, we should think of developing nations as consumers lining up for a greater share of the world's resources.

The advanced nations cannot justify their exclusive and unlimited consumption of the world's resources simply because of their industrial capacity. They should instead use their skills and knowledge to help developing countries modernize, at the same time that they search for ways to reduce their own consumption of resources and lessen the burden on the environment, while maintaining the prosperity of their societies.

The advanced nations must allot a larger portion of economic resources to developing countries. In this way, Japan must make self-control the core of its corporate activities. After all, we are all citizens of one planet, coexisting in the limited space called Earth.

2

CORPORATIONS IN SOCIETY

The Need for Corporate
Self-Control

I mmediately after World War II, the American Occupation
broke up the large Japanese industrial combines, leaving
only small or medium-sized companies in operation.
Through intense competition in a free market system (and special government measures intended to protect designated
industries) and riding the dynamic wave of economic growth,
these companies built the industrial powerhouse that is Japan
today. In time, Japanese corporations grew to the point where
they ranked with the world leaders in their fields.

When such companies were still operating on a small scale
and were concentrating only on their own survival and development, their activities were in basic accord with the good of
the whole country. If that hadn't been the case, there would
have been no reason to tolerate their existence. However, some
companies and corporate cartels grew to gigantic proportions
and achieved near-oligopolistic power, and they sometimes
had a detrimental influence. Oblivious to the damage they
could cause, such companies used their economic might only
for their own gain. In the management of many large companies, the old concept of "profit for the public good" began to

disappear. When that happens, giantism and oligopoly become undesirable elements in the business world.

Up to this moment, the problems associated with their massive size have been considered internal matters for the corporations, but from now on the implications of these problems for society at large will increasingly emerge. Giant business concerns will have to regulate themselves to ensure that they are acting in the interests of the general public. Otherwise, the big corporation will become an antisocial force acting against public interests.

When even the finest managers are suddenly thrust into the position of president or director of a huge company, they may start to see their job as one of protecting the corporation's power and profit. The notion of "profit for the public good" somehow falls by the wayside. Instead, every judgment is based on a much narrower standard: what is best for our company?

Some of these big companies try to move beyond their traditional business bases into any and every line of industry. "To make the most efficient use of our unrivaled management resources, we need to expand through industrial diversification"—that's the standard justification for getting into all kinds of new business lines. Is this kind of diversification a sign of energy and dynamism? Is this trend something to be praised? I don't think so. Rather, I think you could put it this way: Is this kind of diversification another sign that management wants to maximize profits without giving any thought to the social ramifications of its actions?

In my view, giant corporations should hesitate before jumping willy-nilly into new areas of production. A company with a long history behind it will have available the management resources, knowledge, personnel, capital, real estate, and so on, that a new entry in the industry couldn't possibly assemble. It's downright unfair for a big corporation with its low-cost structure to jump into a new market area and start competing with medium-sized or small firms. If we permit this sort of thing, then small companies or new ventures will never have a chance. When a giant company's actions are based on the selfish motive of more profit, it is just like a giant tree in the forest that grows so large that it deprives the vegetation below it of sunlight, so that everything dies.

As a company increases in size, such irresponsible actions can have a huge impact on society and the global economy. That is why large corporations must always be aware of the consequences of their actions. The strongest feature of capitalism is the way it promotes free and fair competition. For that very reason, large players in the market must always apply self-control. In doing so, they must also be aware of the basis of their own existence, for if they think only of increasing profits and enhancing their power—and thus act contrary to the public good—there will always be a backlash that will threaten the corporation's survival. That's exactly what happened in Japan's "bubble economy" of the late 1980s, when companies concerned only with greater profit and more growth went way overboard in the race to increase investments and develop new products.

What We Learn from Nature
Capitalism is based on the principle of free competition, but in order for this principle to work, it is incumbent on economic entities—particularly the strongest and richest—to exercise self-control. As Adam Smith put it, "A man [must have] an impartial spectator inside himself, who calmly watches and criticizes." The same idea has been expressed in the *Analects of Confucius*: "Do not do unto others what you would not have them do unto you." In other words, unless each player in the economy has a clear grasp of the basic principle of self-control, it will become impossible to maintain a free and fair society. This applies particularly to the largest economic players.

In any company, it is tempting to stick to the same management strategy that led the firm from a small beginning to resounding success. However, succeeding managers must realize that the best way is not necessarily just to follow what was done before. What is really needed is giving thought and consideration to the following questions: Should we keep pursuing the goal of getting bigger, and should we continue to aim for endless growth? It may be good for our bottom line, but is it really in the public interest? It is my opinion that if managers don't ask themselves this kind of question and don't exercise the necessary self-control, the healthy development of Japan's economy as a whole will be endangered.

When the United States government deregulated the airline industry, Pan American, one of America's most famous companies, was forced into bankruptcy. The United States government viewed this as a normal business occurrence and engaged in no heroic measures to save the company. Nor did the American people demand such action.

In Japan, though, a situation like this could never have happened. As a general principle, the collapse of any large company is considered a shock to Japanese society. Most likely, the media would blame the government for the business failure; the government, in turn, would consult with industry representatives and then come up with a pot of public money to revive the corporate corpse.

The fact is, though, it is not always a bad thing when a large firm goes bankrupt. Consider the natural world. To any outsider, a forest may look like a stable, peaceful environment, but within it a constant life-and-death drama is being played out among the various types of vegetation. A tall, strong tree will not be tall and strong forever. At some point its vitality will end—and it will fall. And in the open space where it once stood, sunlight will reach the young saplings that had previously been doomed to die in the darkness of the great tree's shade. Those saplings represent the forest's new generation, and they will eventually grow to fill the space left empty by the old tree. Through this harsh process of renewal and regeneration, the forest constantly stays lush and vibrant.

In the same way, large companies tend to die as well—making way for young upstarts that will create new wealth. Through this sometimes harsh process, society gets new bursts of energy that benefit the public. Antitrust laws were written to stave off the harmful effects of monopolies or of excessive size in the business world, but in Japan these laws have not been strictly enforced.

Therefore, instead of arrogantly flaunting its own strength, the proper behavior for a large corporation is to exercise self-restraint, to compete fairly as one player in the free economy, and to act in the best interests of society as a whole. No matter how big the company, the public will only tolerate its existence as long as its operations serve the general good. Management that ignores public interest is inevitably heading for disaster.

From a Closed Corporate Society to an Open One
Around many Japanese companies there has grown up a tightly knit collection of companies that act in concert. This kind of combine, known as a *"keiretsu,"* is a common arrangement in Japan, where society places such importance on groups and connections. In the West, such a combine would be called a "semi-cartel." When American business people come to Japan to try to sell their products, they find that Japanese companies are not exactly lining up to buy, because in the Japanese system each company buys as much as possible from suppliers that are members of its own *keiretsu*. This is not to say that there is a firm rule, or even a cultural requirement, for companies to act this way, but by and large the *keiretsu* do act like cartels. This practice affords mutual protection to members of the *keiretsu*, and it also means that any outsiders will be excluded. Therefore, genuine competition is, in fact, very limited. This is the basic contention of American firms struggling to gain entry into the Japanese market.

I once had the same experience as these Americans. When I founded Kyocera, it was so small that no major manufacturers would have anything to do with me. Out of necessity, I began doing business with American firms.

The *keiretsu* practice also explains the mystery surrounding the strong yen of recent years. Logically, when Japan's currency is strong, prices should go down for consumers because Japanese companies can buy supplies much more cheaply overseas. In fact, the strong yen did not give consumers this boon because domestic companies kept on buying from their domestic *keiretsu* partners.

Once you realize this situation, it is impossible to deny the basic validity of America's complaints about Japan's market. However, the problem isn't limited to the *keiretsu*, and there are many segments of Japanese society where a closed system still exists, making free and fair competition impossible.

It is now obvious to everyone, for example, that the Japanese construction industry is completely locked up, with the work shared out through various *"dango,"* or "arrangements"—that is, private conspiracies to rig the bidding. The finance industry, of course, is also controlled down to the smallest detail by the guidance (actually, regulation) of the Ministry of Finance. The banking industry, too, has worked out various divisions of the business so that no existing bank can fail and new banks can only get started with great difficulty. Because our domestic energy industry has agreed to divide the market in the same way, Japanese consumers pay extremely high rates for electricity.

The industry reputed to be the most backward of all is that of distribution and retailing. Through the Large-scale Retail Store Law, medium and even tiny businesses are protected against competition from bigger and more efficient firms. In freight and delivery as well, existing firms are protected from severe competition by the strong hand of government regulators. In short, there are still many industries where "administrative guidance" by the government protects existing industrial groups and perpetuates the closed nature of Japanese business.

In these ways, the closed corporate society of Japan serves to preserve and protect the interests of existing big corporations and manufacturers. Whether in the domestic or the overseas market, it is extremely hard for a new start-up to break in. Of course, once you become a member of one of these you-scratch-my-back-and-I'll-scratch-yours corporate arrangements, you can manage your company predictably and securely.

There is a downside to the *keiretsu* arrangement, which is that a corporation can be so bound by the group's way of doing things that it becomes difficult to come up with any innovative ideas. This is particularly true when the economy is weak. Because protecting the established order is the top priority of the *keiretsu*, it is almost impossible for members to embark on new lines of business. The resulting danger is that the company's entrepreneurial zeal will dissipate and vanish.

In an open society, companies will usually be subjected to tough competition. To prevail in the competition, a company will need new ideas, new products, and better product development skills. And that means companies will have to buy the best materials and supplies available—even if these come from suppliers that are outside the buyer's *keiretsu*. Starting with these materials, the company must apply its own creativity to add value and develop unique, quality goods. A company that can marshal creative resources in this way has the ability to develop new markets of its own. It therefore remains strong even when the overall economy is weak.

Some managers insist that the closed industrial system is necessary in order to protect smaller, weaker firms. This justification, in fact, gets it completely back to front. Japan's closed economy exists to serve the largest companies and ensure that they continue to dominate smaller suppliers and subcontractors. At any time, in any line of business, the basic industrial structure of Japan centers on the big players. And their attitude toward small fry is essentially "to hell with you." Since the basic goal is to preserve the existing structure, this is a very different matter from the protection of small businesses, no matter how much the big companies may claim that this is the reason. Rather, under the guise of helping the weak, the strong companies have simply created a system that is primarily useful to themselves.

In Japan's present mature economy, with consumers' needs increasing, I am firmly convinced that the healthy development of Japan's future economy requires a more open corporate structure. Japan's economy will surely spring to life when the companies that have won public support in free and fair competition are the ones that continue to experience growth.

Thus, the purpose for reforms that will give Japan an open corporate structure is not just to eliminate business friction, or to increase imports from overseas. Instead, the main purpose is to ensure the continued healthy development of Japan's economy.

Fair Corporate Management Through Openness
No matter how free a society may be, a business entity can never have unlimited freedom. As I have repeatedly said, its activities must be regulated so that it serves the public. However, a sound market economy cannot be based on that alone.

To avoid public suspicion of corporate activities, corporate managers must operate in the public eye—that is, they must preserve a basic visibility in all they do. Society has to act as a check to ensure that powerful companies do not use their might simply for the enrichment of a small clique of insiders, or work against the temper of the times and the public good, or make illegal deals with politicians or bureaucrats.

Corporations are divided into various sections and departments. An outsider might have all the basic financial data about a particular firm but still not realize exactly what is going on inside. For this reason, a system called "disclosure of information by segment," in which each section of a company releases detailed information about its own operations, has become standard operating procedure in American and European companies, being judged to be the best way to protect the interests of stockholders and directors.

In Japan, even among companies that have been progressive about releasing information, there are differences of opinion about this system of "disclosure of information by segment." Those opposing the release of more information argue simply that companies need some secrets. If every plan and strategy is laid bare for all to see, they say, the company will be placed at a competitive disadvantage, and that will be costly to stockholders. In fact, though, this business about "costly to stockholders" suggests a rather short-term view of costs and benefits; it completely ignores the interests of the general public—the people who may well become the future stockholders of the company.

Particularly in a large corporation, whose operations can have a huge impact on society, it can be all but impossible for outsiders to understand what management is up to. It is time for large corporations, in response to public demand, to take the initiative and move toward the "disclosure of information by segment" system so that the management of these enterprises can be carried out in the public view. It seems to me that this system of reporting is an important part of the basic rationale of a corporation. The very origins of democratic society stem from the notion that enterprises are managed fairly. It follows that, no matter what the particulars of a company's organization, public access to corporate information is important—and becomes more so as the company gets larger.

From the point of view of the public good, it is necessary for this openness to be established as a basic management principle. It is particularly important for a company whose shares are traded publicly in a capitalist economy to work positively toward open information to ensure the sound growth of the stock market. Through the release of corporate information, right down to the departmental level, anybody who examines it will be able to judge how fairly management is operating. I believe that this is in the best interests of shareholders, directors, and the general public.

When every corporation adopts an open information policy to the fullest possible extent, so that every company can be easily seen to be managed properly, the healthy growth of Japan's economy can continue, and lingering distrust can be eliminated.

Independent Small Businesses Will Change Japan

The rapid growth of postwar Japan was the result of hard work by small and medium-sized businesses. After all, it was from these small companies that the nation's giant firms grew. With close ties to the government and protected by government regulations, they developed into the corporate monoliths that now dominate their industries. That gave rise to the current situation, where whole industries are structured chiefly to preserve the rank and privileges of these giants.

The companies that remained small have generally been reduced to the status of subcontractors for the giants—and have lost much of their own initiative in the process. As long as the existing industrial structure is maintained, Japan's economy will remain weak and passive. As I have said already, a smooth exchange of positions between old and new companies is essential to maintain the dynamism of an economy.

To make sure that happens, small business managers need to combine the zeal of the entrepreneur with the patience to make skillful decisions, for the simple truth is that it is the small and medium-sized businesses that are supporting the Japanese economy right now.

The small and medium-sized business sector represents more than 99 percent of all Japanese companies and accounts for 80 percent of all jobs. The vitality of the nation depends on these small vibrant companies, from which the next generation of corporations will spring. The "Seiwa Juku" seminars, which I will discuss next, were set up to help those companies.

Fourteen years ago, in the spring of 1983, I received a request from some young managers of small businesses in Kyoto to arrange an opportunity for them to study my ideas on management and my philosophy of life. As a result of that request, the "Seiwa Juku" seminars, which are a kind of study group, came about.

I began giving these enthusiastic young executives my answers to their questions, such as "What is management?" and "What kind of person should a manager be?" In time, requests for similar sessions came in from all over the country, and the number of seminars grew rapidly. Up to 1996, more than 3,000 executives from all parts of Japan have attended more than 150 sessions of the Seiwa Juku. I'm doing this on a voluntary basis, and as long as I have enough energy I plan to continue conducting these seminars so that I can meet as many young managers as possible and share my ideas with them.

As far as I am concerned, the small business managers constitute the real elite of the nation—not the politicians, bureaucrats, or scholars. The reason is plain: they sacrifice their whole lives and give their all to the company in order to make sure that their company's employees and their families have a good life. And my wish for them is that they become even more outstanding human beings.

It goes without saying that in any organization the people at the top bear final responsibility. They are indispensable. This is particularly true of a small or medium-sized business. If the top person loses interest, or his attention is distracted, the company will immediately suffer. My goal is to work with the managers who bear this heavy responsibility and help them achieve a correct and beneficial philosophy. In this way, they will be able to improve the lives of employees and their families and expand their businesses so they can begin to shoulder greater responsibilities to work for the betterment of international society. Through this, Japan will become a finer country and a better place to live.

The Seiwa Juku seminar was not established to pass along nuts-and-bolts management know-how. Instead, I try to focus on the bigger picture: the right frame of mind for a manager, and the correct course of a human life. And when those lessons are done, we tend to go out as a group, to eat and drink and carry the conversation further. In this way, through the Seiwa Juku seminar I have passed on my ideas at locations throughout Japan.

The attendees themselves—people who are responsible for the operation of their own companies—listen carefully to what I say, and the results have been satisfying. Most of the companies represented at the seminars have reported good results, even in the current recession. It's almost unbelievable how many people report back to me after the seminar that their company performances have improved. That's why I decided—in the hope of contributing a little bit to the revitalization of the economy—to dedicate most of the rest of my life to the Seiwa Juku seminar.

Toward Management That Satisfies the Public

What is the role of the corporation in society? That is easy to answer. It is to engage in activities that please its customers and the general public. Some fifteen years ago, I founded Japan's second long-distance telephone company, known as "Daini Denden," meaning "The Second Telegraph and Telephone Company." Today, the firm is generally known by its initials, DDI. In 1993, our annual sales totaled US$2.3 billion and our operating profits reached US$240 million. By 1996, our annual sales had grown to US$4.7 billion, and operating profits totaled US$576 million. In the stock market, by the end of 1995 the company reached an impressive total capitalization of US$19 billion.

The success of a company that provides only a small reduction in long-distance telephone charges was due entirely to the fact that the venture was based from the start on an ideal: to do something good for the general public. It's clear that the company found the right time and the right way to be useful to society. I will discuss my entry into the long-distance telephone business in the third part of this book.

The members of the group that started DDI were total neo-phytes in the communications business. The business press and financial analysts thought we were crazy to challenge NTT (Nippon Telegraph and Telephone Corporation), Japan's powerful telephone monopoly. They all agreed that there was no way we could expect to succeed.

In Japan's industrial world, the most common arrangement for starting up a huge project like this would be for the giants in the industry to form a joint venture among themselves. The whole structure of industrial circles is set up that way. However, in this case, if a joint venture between the high and mighty had been formed, it would have produced only a replica of the existing giant, NTT. And a company as big and inefficient as that could not have provided lower long-distance telephone rates for Japan's consumers. I felt that if just one company—even one run by a bunch of communications amateurs—could get into the business with the pure motivation of providing cheaper long-distance telephone service, it would spawn genuine competition that would inevitably lead to reduced phone rates for consumers. That was my goal when I founded DDI.

Naturally, it wasn't easy. Beyond the technological problems, we had all sorts of difficulties negotiating with the government and so on. However, we put every ounce of our energy into the work because of our wholehearted commitment to the principle of serving the public. And I am convinced that this dedication to the interests of the public was the chief factor behind DDI's success.

I wished very much to spread this ideal around the world, so in 1993 I decided to take part in Motorola's ambitious "Iridium Project," a new approach to cellular telephony. By launching sixty-six dedicated satellites in orbit around the earth, the "Iridium Project" will make it possible to place or receive a telephone call anywhere in the world with a phone that fits in your pocket. Motorola and the Kyocera-DDI group are aiming to have this system in operation by 1998.

Many hurdles remain, and the risks are considerable, but if it works, this project would clearly provide important benefits to people all over the world—particularly in Africa, Eastern Europe, the Middle East, and Central America, where communications are not as advanced and it is more difficult to make long-distance telephone calls.

So far I have discussed several of my business projects. One factor that is common to all of them is that, no matter how hard you work, every successful company has to be built around the ideal of providing some good to customers and to the nation. If that ideal is present from the beginning, it will provide a framework for all subsequent corporate strategies. No matter how innovative a company's technology may be, no matter how meticulous its planning, a company cannot succeed without this basic ideal.

Chapter 5

The Role of the Government

I have spent my whole life as a technician and business manager. Therefore, when it comes to government and public administration, I am a complete novice. At the end of 1990, I had a chance conversation with the late Eiji Suzuki, chairman of Mitsubishi Kasei Corporation (now Mitsubishi Chemical Corporation). He had been named chairman of the Provisional Council for the Promotion of Administrative Reform, which was more popularly known as the third "Administrative Reform Council," or ARC. He told me that he would like to have me chair the section of his council charged with studying the theme, "Japan and the World."

Between running Kyocera and starting up DDI, I was one extremely busy person. Yet I was also someone with the privileged background of starting a company in Japan and seeing it become a success, and I had been wondering if there was some way I could pay back some of the debt I felt I owed the nation. After thinking long and hard, I decided that despite being a total neophyte on the subject, I would give it a try.

For about the first two years of the ARC's life, it was divided into three major sections. Former Prime Minister Morihiro Hosokawa chaired the section on the issue of "A Prosperous Lifestyle"; former Supreme Court Chief Justice Reijiro Tsunoda chaired the committee on "Fair and Transparent Administrative Procedure"; and I was in charge of "Japan and the World."

My section included a broad list of questions and concerns, ranging from the huge (encompassing the basic aims of Japan's foreign policy, ODA [Official Development Assistance], global environmental protection, and so on) to the minute (the optimum period of validity for a passport or driver's license, the bureaucracy's shift to using A4 size paper, etc.). In some of these areas, I do feel that in a small way we may have provided a useful service to the people of Japan.

My committee concluded its work in June of 1992, with the issue of a report, an excerpt of which is included at the end of this chapter. After that date, the ARC was divided into two larger groups. One dealt with changing administrative operating procedures to set up clear channels of authority, and the other focused on "A Re-examination of the Role of Government." Tapped again by Chairman Suzuki, my role—right up until October 1993, when the third ARC came to an end—was to run the subcommittee on "A Re-examination of the Role of Government."

This turned out to be a hard and trying task. For one thing, just as we were about to write our report on administrative enterprises and special public corporations, the famous parliamentary election of 1993 took place, when the voters threw out the Liberal Democratic Party that had ruled Japan for forty straight years. This result in itself clearly suggested that a major "re-examination of government" was already under way. In addition, we came under enormous pressure from the various agencies of the bureaucracy and from politicians representing interest groups who supported the agencies.

The experience nevertheless allowed me the opportunity to work closely with Japanese bureaucrats for three years. And it was in this way that this neophyte got a close look at how the bureaucratic system actually works. I regard it as a very valuable learning experience.

From my first days on the ARC, I had some doubts as to whether the council was in a position to achieve anything. Its members were supposed to review mountains of literature, listen to bureaucrats and experts in various fields, and then draw up a proposal for a new bureaucratic system. We were then to deliver our proposals to a small decision-making circle within the prime minister's cabinet. However, before our reports could be presented at that meeting, we had to obtain the agreement of all the relevant government agencies. This required a series of compromises, and little by little we found ourselves bogged down in a quagmire.

Eventually, the reports that emerged from this process were delivered to the Prime Minister's Office. The cabinet then declared that the recommendations would be treated as "matters of the greatest importance." This was the fate of the work of the Administrative Reform Council.

In fact, many of these "matters of the greatest importance" never went anywhere. And if that turns out to be the fate of most recommendations of the ARC, then all the members' contributions and hard work were a waste of time. In my view, there is no evidence that the ARC can play any role in our present political system, or that any reform council can achieve anything. After three years of hard work, it has become clear that the "reform council" approach to bureaucratic change is severely limited. In the future, the members of Japan's Diet, or parliament, should study the matter themselves and act on their own initiative. New legislation, written without the need for constant negotiations with bureaucrats, is the only way that drastic reforms will ever be achieved.

There was another sizable problem as well. For the most part, the ARC committees held their hearings at the various agencies they were investigating. Naturally, when the bureaucrats appeared to testify on the situation in their own ministries, they all said essentially the same thing: "Everything is in order. There are no problems here." As one person who sat through it all observed, this was the equivalent of calling in a physician and then telling him, "Actually, Doctor, there's nothing wrong with me."

During the time I was working with the bureaucrats, I found that this was precisely their attitude. In the world of the government official, although mistakes may be made now and then, it is taboo to admit to them. The agencies simply do not tolerate anyone suggesting that their policies may have been wrong. All of us have been taught from childhood that the only way to make progress is to learn from our mistakes and try to avoid them in the future, but this piece of common sense has not yet penetrated the mind of the bureaucrat.

This explains the stubborn bureaucratic resistance to any efforts at reform. After all, if you have never done anything that requires correcting, if the social and industrial order you have created is perfect, then there's nothing that needs to be reformed. The problem with this mindset is that we live in times of radical changes. In these circumstances, it is a basic truth that the policies that were appropriate in the past need to be re-examined to see if they still apply.

Even more surprising is the way the bureaucrats place restrictions on freedom of speech. To make sure that members felt free to express their views candidly, the meetings of the ARC were always private. And yet, all the time I was on the ARC, I noticed that whenever I said anything critical about a particular ministry, I would get a phone call from that ministry the following morning.

"Most honorable Mr. Inamori," the caller would say, "you obviously have an unfortunate misunderstanding about what we are doing, so I would like to offer a respectful explanation." And then the explanation would flow forth—proving that the ministry was proceeding in precisely the correct manner. This would continue until I finally had to say, "Yes, I understand."

In that kind of stifling atmosphere, it is obvious that dissenting opinions will never come out. Although it is a truism that any situation will look different from different points of view, it is germane to the democratic process to respect opinions arising from various points of view and to consider all the conflicting opinions and come to a decision. Yet, this process is totally ignored and not permitted within the bureaucracy.

Another thing I came to recognize on the ARC was the mysterious language called "bureaucratese." For example, when a bureaucrat looks you in the eye and says "I will give the matter careful study," what he's really saying is "I won't do a damn thing about it."

The most bureaucratic expression of all must surely be "*sawasarinagara*," which is an old samurai word, a fancy way of saying "You're right up to a point, but..." The bureaucrats use this to mean, "As a general principle, the point you are making is certainly accurate and I respect it fully, but in the specific area under my jurisdiction, your assertion would, of course, not apply."

This "*sawasarinagara*" has a multitude of nuances. Essentially, it is used to cover up what is really happening—that is, while the bureaucrat is pretending to be sympathetic to the person he's dealing with, his real goal is to protect his own interests. There are many occasions when bureaucrats may listen to what somebody from the outside is saying—but do not really hear a word of it. Yes, I came to came to gain many insights through working with bureaucrats.

From countless such exchanges with government officials, I came away convinced that even though they, too, are Japanese and they, too, are working within a democracy, there is some fundamental difference between us, some basic discrepancy in the way we view human nature.

Through my work on the ARC I had the opportunity to meet and get to know a large number of bureaucrats. It seemed to me that they had become, in a sense, captives of their own organizations and could speak only as mouthpieces for those organizations. Nevertheless, as individuals, many of them are extremely dedicated, splendid people, as well as very knowledgeable. If you could only just pry them away from their organizations, they could be a veritable treasure house of all that is good in mankind.

Public Administration for the Public

Since the beginning of the Meiji era in the late 1860s, the nation has based its development on a platform borrowed from the West. One of the most effective of the Western elements that was adopted was the centralization of power to guide the nation as a whole. At the core of this centralized government is the bureaucracy.

After Japan's defeat in the World War II, virtually all national institutions, both political and industrial, were radically reformed. The military was disbanded, the Constitution completely rewritten, the financial community born anew. However, the central bureaucracy continued basically unchanged, except for some minor organizational rearrangements here and there. It goes without saying that this strong central bureaucracy was a key factor in nurturing Japan into the economic giant it has become, despite various setbacks along the way. At the same time, it is also true that the bureaucracy played a key role in creating Japan's closed economic system that has been criticized around the world.

Japan's bureaucrats are imbued with the self-assurance that it was they who built, and will preserve, modern Japan, and there should not be anybody else thinking about what's best for the country. And this is why they will not tolerate any criticism of their actions from the private sector.

In fact, it's really not enough to describe the system as "a strong centralized bureaucracy." What the bureaucrats have created is a "bureautocracy"—a government of the bureaucrats, for the bureaucrats, and by the bureaucrats. This is completely different from the way democracy works in Europe or the United States. The vaunted "sovereignty of the people" established by Japan's postwar Constitution has somehow disappeared.

However, the central government officials who established this strong "bureautocracy" are now paying a high price for their refusal to heed criticism. The result of their insistence on doing things their way, and only their way, is that they have lost the vitality necessary to reform themselves. In a rapidly changing world, a bureaucracy that refuses to change will eventually be left behind by the rest of society. It's a case of inevitable fatigue. In any case, now that Japan has grown to the position of the world's second-richest country, the bureaucracy has fully achieved its original postwar goals. Now that its job done, do we need this institution any more?

Private companies, after all, have had to learn new ways of operating, particularly in the severe recession of recent years. Top managers have had to pare down their organizations to increase efficiency and productivity. And yet the bureaucracy, funded with taxpayers' money, has continued to grow—even as the national economy is floundering. It's a perfect example of Parkinson's Law at work.

The system of national administration and the bureaucracy were originally intended to enhance the public good. They were established to make Japan a better place for the general public—in accordance with the Constitution's establishment of popular sovereignty. Isn't it time now to return to this original purpose? To do that, we need to examine, case by case, whether this ever-growing bureaucracy is really useful to the general public. And if we decide it is not, we need to do some radical cutting back. In other words, we have to jettison our "bureautocracy" and replace it with a genuine democracy. This is what the Japanese people are asking for. It is also what the rest of the world is demanding as well.

A Bureaucratic System Puts Bureaucrats First

When I was twenty-seven years old, I developed a new type of ceramic with special electronic properties, and I then set up Kyocera Corporation to manufacture and sell this new technology. As the electronics industry began to experience huge growth in the semiconductor business, I continued in my career as a manager in the technological field. Accordingly, I had little contact with Japan's bureaucrats. As the field of ceramics technology was then completely new, the bureaucrats were basically unaware of it and therefore it did not fall within the jurisdiction of any of the ministries. Meanwhile, at Kyocera, we were fervently engaged in perfecting our technology and extending its applications, and we put all our efforts into facing the rigors of open global competition. Concepts like monopolies or the formation of cartels never crossed our minds. We were focused heart and soul on developing and producing goods that could compete in the world marketplace.

That all changed when I got involved in developing DDI, the long-distance telephone company. This was an area that was heavily regulated by the government, and we found ourselves buried in a sea of rules and red tape. These excessive regulations, I can frankly say, do not exist for the good of the public. The only purpose they serve is to increase the power of the respective ministries and give the bureaucrats some justification for their existence. By enforcing all of its many rules, each division of each bureau of each ministry can protect its administrative turf, augment its power, and protect its budget. Each department swaggers about, confident in the weight of its own authority, behaving as though the ministry itself—or, for that matter, the whole nation—didn't matter. For each agency, of course, the extent of its jurisdiction is directly related to its power, and naturally nobody feels any incentive to decrease his own power.

The most important factor in this closed world is "consensus." Individual opinion is of no consequence, and superiors who have risen through the ranks have no interest in proposals from subordinates. It is a system, in short, where everyone has decided things will work better if there is no leadership. Rather, the responsibility for making and carrying out policy lies with the division-chief class of bureaucrats, men who are in their forties. When you closely examine the system they have risen up through, I sincerely doubt that many of them are capable of looking out for the long-term interests of the state.

For the average citizen, "the state" is not really a concrete entity but a rather vague concept. And in countless ways these bureaucrats govern "the state" and dominate and dictate to the populace. In fact, these people whose job it is to enforce the statutes and impose their interpretation of the law on the public are often younger than most of the population. These are the "best and the brightest" of the young—people with enough brains to graduate from Tokyo University (essentially, Harvard, Yale, and Princeton rolled into one) and pass the infamously rigorous public service entrance examination. However, just because they have been marked out for the elite track since childhood and have never suffered a setback does not make them any wiser than the ordinary working person. And it certainly doesn't guarantee that they will never make mistakes.

The bureaucratic species will routinely seek to carry on in the same old decision-by-consensus, promotion-by-seniority style. If there is no consensus, the bureaucrats begin to feel insecure and so they cling to this "bureaucracy first" system— and the politicians, the media, and the business world all go along without a word of complaint. Of course, it is also true that even after their government careers are over, some bureaucrats plan to make the so-called *ama-kudari*—literally, "descent from heaven," the Japanese term for the revolving-door syndrome, where a top bureaucrat leaves his ministry and goes to work for the industry he once regulated.

In today's rapidly changing world, foreign nations want to

see Japan formulate and implement a clear foreign policy. Domestically as well, the people in our increasingly prosperous consumer nation are looking for new policies. At a time when both the nation and the world are seeing a climate of major change, the public expects the bureaucrats to forge a changed Japan for changing times.

APPENDIX

An extract from "Basic Principles of Japanese External Policy," from the "First Report on Administrative Reform," submitted to the Prime Minister on July 4, 1991, by the Provisional Council for the Promotion of Administrative Reform, approved by the Government on July 9, 1991 (published by the Management and Coordination Agency, November 1991).

1) Freedom and Democracy

A free, democratic society is a society tolerant to all, open to all, allowing participation by all who have the ability and will to do so, having fair rules and realizing social justice, and promoting the independence of its members.

Freedom and democracy are principles that a society must strive every day to achieve. In this sense, they are universal principles, and Japan must begin by applying them thoroughly at home.

Only through increasing our recognition thereof can freedom and democracy have true meaning as principles of our external policy.

2) Pacifism

The Preamble to the Japanese Constitution states: "We, the Japanese people, desire peace for all time.... We recognize that all peoples of the world have the right to live in peace, free from fear and want." The pacifism espoused by our Constitution is thus not a "one-country pacifism" that claims: "It's all right as long as Japan is at peace" or "Everything is fine as long as we are not involved in warfare." The pacifism in the Japanese Constitution calls on us to work within the international community to maintain and create peace throughout the world.

We must be aware that patient efforts are required in the course of achieving this pacifism. We should therefore extend the utmost cooperation, to the fullest extent that our Constitution permits, when peace is disrupted and the international community moves to restore it.

3) International Cooperation
The Preamble to the Japanese Constitution states that "no nation is responsible to itself alone" and "We desire to occupy an honored place in an international society...." A spirit of international cooperation will only be achieved when each and every individual in Japan recognizes that our country exists within the larger framework of the international community.

As for public administration, it should be conducted in a fair and transparent manner that is convincing from the international perspective, recognizing that the international community watches closely each domestic act by the government. Japan should not trot out special domestic concerns in an attempt to place itself beyond the scope of international rules.

It is even more important, as recognizing Japan in a larger framework of the international community, for us to act based on a spirit of philanthropy and love for all humankind in cooperation with the rest of the world. We must recognize that Japan was able to rise from the ruins of the war and achieve the economic prosperity it enjoys today owing greatly to, under international cooperation, the relatively stable international order in the postwar era and the support of the people of the world.

Now that we have successfully achieved economic prosperity, it is only right that we approach the world in a spirit of philanthropy and love for all humankind, that we use our economic and other abilities to contribute to the world around us, even if it means incurring some sacrifices ourselves. We need to state clearly that in Japan since ancient times has existed the spirit of working for the good of the world and for the good of one's fellows.

4) Contributions to Mankind
Japan must, furthermore, build on the principles espoused in its

Constitution and take a further step in contributing to the solution of common issues of mankind, which were not really conceived when the Constitution was adopted.

Japan should make active contributions in such areas as the protection of the global environment, the overcoming of the population explosion, the solution of the energy problem, the fostering of the development of science, technology, scholarship—which are the common assets of humankind—and the promotion of respect for various cultures in the world.

Chapter

6

Creating a Truly Free Society

L ooking back in history, Japan's first written code of laws
was the Taiho Legal Code, set forth in 701 A.D. It was
hardly the equivalent of modern law, but in basic out-
line it was not unlike our contemporary code. Its eleven vol-
umes of statutes were intended—like modern regulations—to
preserve social order. In other words, even 1,300 years ago,
Japan had a plethora of rules and regulations to control the
populace.

Ever since then, Japan has had a national government
headed by the emperor. The truth about our system of "imperial rule," however, is that the emperors have rarely had much
to do with actually governing the people. Rather, jurisdiction
over people's lives has been exercised in the emperor's name
by a council or some other form of bureaucracy. This kind of
governmental arrangement encouraged people to view bureaucrats as "honorable superiors," a feeling that survives to
this day.

The Meiji reformers, who brought Japan into the modern
era at the end of the nineteenth century, replaced the feudal
structure of government with a system of government by cabi-

net. Naturally, this had all the appearance of being new and modern, but at heart it was once again based on a strong centralized government system. In Meiji times, the government's overriding mission was to catch up with, and surpass, the advanced nations of the West. For that purpose, people of great talent and intelligence were called into government service, and in time the government became extremely powerful.

Japan's defeat in World War II marked the end of imperial government. Under the postwar Constitution, the emperor has been relegated to being a mere symbol, and a democratic government, based on the doctrine of the sovereignty of the people, has been established. In such a system, the bureaucracy is supposed to be the servant rather than the ruler of the people—and government officials should be known as "public servants," a term borrowed from the West. This change came about when I was in junior high school.

Of course, the officials, who had considered themselves "honorable superiors," were shocked to be told they were now servants—that is, public servants. It seemed to indicate a revolutionary change. However, the bureaucrats did not settle passively into their new role. In the years after World War II, a time of chaotic change and confusion in Japanese society, the bureaucrats had to take the lead in re-establishing social stability—and in the blink of an eye the "honorable superiors" were back again, issuing orders to control the public. On the premise that they could stabilize society better than the private sector, the bureaucrats gradually cast their regulatory net farther, using their power of permit and certification to enhance their authority. All the time people were talking about deregulation, the number and the scope of regulations just kept increasing. And the price for this was that the ideal of a government that trusted the people, that let each individual work to improve his standard of living, and that gave the people sovereignty and made the bureaucrats their "public servants" got lost along the way.

As the bureaucrats perceived it, they had a responsibility to watch, to guide, and to regulate peoples' lives from A to Z. They simply did not trust the public with the freedom to run their lives by themselves. It was their attitude that the populace needed to be protected, whether they knew it or not.

One can see this attitude clearly, for example, in the relationship between the Ministry of Transport, Japan's version of the United States' Department of Transportation, and the airline industry. The airline companies are not permitted to set their own fares. In fact, though, each airline's cost and operating structures are different, and passengers should be able to choose among the different levels of service offered. Fares should be left up to the individual companies.

The same situation applies to government regulation of the airwaves. The air does not belong to the government—it is the people's, but of course broadcasting has come under government control. Why can't there be more freedom for broadcasters who want to use the FM band or create cable TV networks. At present, the number of FM radio stations and cable TV stations in Japan is much lower than in Western countries. Why can't individuals who can assemble the necessary technical skill and capital have the right to get into this business with minimal control from the government?

The extensive regulation of Japan's finance and banking industry is much the same. Existing regulations have nothing to do with the service given to consumers, which is why banking is so much less convenient in Japan than in the United States or Europe. We have seen some degree of deregulation in this industry recently, but it still makes you wonder why Japanese banks have such restricted hours, why the ATM machines can't be used at night, why you can do certain banking chores on the machines on weekdays but can't do them on the same machines on Saturday. Why not give customers what they want?

Who is paying for this unnecessary bureaucratic interference? The ordinary citizen, of course. This is the basic reason why it is commonly said that Japan is a rich country, but the Japanese are not rich people. Japan has become a place where the ruling bureaucrats simply ignore the interests of the public.

Fixing the Price Gap to Improve the Quality of Life

In the years just after Japan's defeat in World War II, the developed countries of the world—primarily the United States—opened their markets and willingly imported Japanese goods so that Japan, a nation that survives by trade, was able to grow as the global market grew. And Japan did prosper.

Now Japan has to ask whether a country that has become so strong through manufacturing really needs to protect its domestic markets and manufacturers against foreign competitors. Personally, I can't agree with the argument that Japan is some unique entity that needs special rules. In my view, a world economic superpower should open its markets and take on all competition. If it doesn't, other countries will eventually start closing their markets to Japan, and the country will no longer be able to develop companies that can compete globally In short, Japan has to change the system where everything and everybody is controlled by one uniform set of rules and pointed toward a single goal. Now that Japan has become a global economic power, that is precisely what other countries fear.

After the so-called Plaza Accord of 1985, when the finance ministers of the major countries met at the Plaza Hotel in New York and agreed to weaken the dollar significantly against the yen, there began a long period when the yen continuously strengthened. Overall, since then the dollar has fallen to less than half its former value vis-à-vis the yen. In 1985, US$1.00 would buy goods in Japan worth ¥250. Today, it would take about US$2.40 to buy the same goods.

This change had two practical implications. First, it undermined the global competitiveness of Japanese goods. Since a Japanese product that used to cost US$1.00 in the United States now costs US$2.40, it is much harder to sell Japanese exports. Second, imported products coming into Japan have become much cheaper for Japanese consumers: an import that would have cost ¥240 in 1985 now costs only ¥100. Since imported goods can be sold much more cheaply, Japanese consumers should have seen a major improvement in their quality of life; in a word, they should be richer.

In the face of this severe competition in sales, Japan's exporting companies have been working their fingers to the bone for years now—and they have somehow managed to survive despite the high yen. However, the high yen has not brought the expected benefits for Japanese consumers. In dollar terms, the Japanese are the richest people on earth today, with a per capita GNP of about US$33,000—some 40 percent higher than the per capita GNP in the United States. Yet the average Japanese feels far from rich. The blame for this situation lies with the bureaucracy: government policies have simply failed to pass on the benefits of the strong yen to the Japanese people.

One place where this is evident is in the vast gap between prices for goods in Japan and prices for the same goods overseas. Japan is often said to be the greatest beneficiary of the global trading system, but this price gap demonstrates that Japan's closed economic system does not serve the best interests of the public, and that our economic policies have not been correct.

According to a 1993 report from the Economic Planning Agency—a government agency somewhat equivalent to the United States' Bureau of Labor Statistics—each 10 percent increase in the value of the yen should bring a saving of ¥3 trillion (about US$30 billion) per year to Japanese consumers. If we look at 1993—when the yen went up by some 20 percent—it follows that Japanese consumers should have been richer to the tune of US$60 billion. In fact, though, a private study in June of 1993 showed that Japanese consumers were paying 44 percent more than New Yorkers for a basket of ordinary food and other daily items.

The Japanese people don't need studies to tell them this. In a nation where 10 million people travel overseas every year, they have seen with their own eyes that prices are much lower abroad, both in nearby Asian countries and in the West. This has, of course, fueled deep feelings of discontent in the public.

The source of this massive price gap is the plethora of unnecessary regulations that are strangling the Japanese market. I am convinced that if Japan could become a country that relied on free market mechanisms rather than regulations, this domestic–overseas price gap could be eliminated almost completely in a few years. From that point on, the citizens of Japan might begin to feel in real life what is now true only on paper—that they are among the richest people on the earth.

Let's Deregulate—and Leave the Decisions to the Public

I do not condemn all government regulations and intervention. Japan's stunning recovery after World War II is, of course, due both to the people's unflagging efforts and to government policies. However, in today's world the nature of the regulations that are required has changed. Japan is no longer a country in which the only industries are small start-ups that need help. Today, corporate Japan includes many of the giants of world industry. In such a dramatically different environment, there is no place for policies that are just a continuation of the past. We need a completely new approach. Instead of exerting constant control over the private sector, the government should trust private citizens and companies to act in their own best interests.

Let us consider the computer industry as a case in point. In 1957, when Japan still lagged well behind the United States and Europe in computer and electronics technology, the Electronic Industry Promotion Law was passed. This national policy resulted from the decision that Japan's domestic makers should be promoted and protected. The results were remarkable and Japanese electronics firms climbed to the top rung of the industry worldwide. In other words, the policy paid off up to that point.

Then, in an era of explosively rapid technological change, new companies like Apple, Compaq, and Sun Microsystems sprang up in the United States, employing creative technologies to produce one innovation after another that appealed to consumers everywhere. In Japan, however, there was no such wave of innovative new start-ups. Why was this?

The reason lies in the Japanese administrative system, which is intended to promote catching up with other countries and is simply not suited for creating new industries. Under the slogan "protect and develop existing industries," the system certainly had a measure of initial success, but eventually it turned into a political-regulatory-corporate triangle aimed at preserving market order and protecting profits. There was nothing about encouraging or helping small new business ventures.

As I have noted many times, Japan's administrators do not trust the private sector. To the contrary, they are certain that market chaos would result if private companies were allowed to operate on their own. The usefulness of that level of regulation has long since ended. In order to see the light at the end of this long recessionary tunnel, we're going to need regulation that encourages dynamism within the economy. To do that, you have to trust people in the private sector and leave business up to them. This is the way competitive entrepreneurs will create new businesses.

When one considers global issues such as the environmental crisis, the North–South wealth gap, and the energy problem, it's clear that Japan's present system, which promotes the growth of large-scale production and large-scale consumption, is no longer desirable. At the very least, Japan's expectations must change.

Corporate managers who have assumed that economic growth would continue indefinitely are going to have to rethink their directions. It may well be that, for the near future, the current pattern of zero growth and zero increases in annual salaries will continue. If that happens, all the vitality will be drained from the system and hope will be destroyed.

The way to avoid this is deregulation, which is an absolute necessity. As I said earlier, with deregulation prices would actually fall from year to year, eventually eliminating the price gap between Japan and overseas countries. Then the man on the street would see an enormous gain in his purchasing power, and the lifestyle of the Japanese would be more prosperous. The elimination of the regulatory protection of a few favored industries would also encourage the appearance of more new industries creating new products and types of business. When an economy has that kind of dynamism, people will be able to increase their wealth even in low- or zero-growth periods.

A clear demonstration of the value of deregulation, and its benefits for the average consumer, can be found in the long-distance telephone market. The three telecommunications reform acts, of which the 1985 Telecommunications Business Law was the first, broke up the monopoly in the communications business and made it a free market.

The result of this move was the creation of three new companies in the long-distance telecommunications market, including DDI Corporation, the company I run. In the ten years since then, the results have been dramatic. A three-minute daytime call from Tokyo to Osaka, for example, has dropped from ¥400 to ¥170. This means that a caller who makes just two 15-minute long-distance telephone calls per week will save about US$1,200 per year. I think it must be admitted that this is more valuable to the average citizen than the small tax cuts we've received recently.

The benefits are not restricted to long-distance telephone

calls. Deregulation of the telecommunications industry has spawned the birth of all sorts of local communications companies and cellular phone companies, all focused on providing new services for customers. For example, DDI and its cellular phone companies are currently investing US$8 billion in the business. In short, the possibilities for the growth of investment and efficiency from here on seem almost incredible.

To summarize, the results of the deregulation of telecommunications have benefited consumers so remarkably that there's simply no comparison with the way things were before. As someone directly involved in the surge of this newly freed market, I am intensely aware of the merits of deregulation.

From Bureaucracy to Independence
Some people feel that, even if some degree of deregulation was achieved, Japan would still need to rely heavily on the skills and expertise of the bureaucrats, or at least work in conjunction with them. However, I don't share this view.

Naturally, the bureaucrats who create and administer the vast panoply of regulations will always argue that there's an important reason for every last clause of the rule book. In actual fact, though, it is rather strange for a democratic country to place such extensive reliance on regulations dispensed by bureaucrats. The bureaucrats are not elected by the people and hold no legislative authority. So I feel their power should be diminished through deregulation and returned to those who are directly elected by the people—the legislators.

Some members of the Diet, or parliament, would probably say something like: "We don't have the technical expertise of the bureaucrats, and we don't have the right policy staff to advise us. (In contrast to the U.S. Congress, members of Japan's Diet maintain a minimal office staff.) In the Japanese system, most rules are not legislated by Diet members but are made by bureaucrats in the appropriate ministry." However, anyone who comes up with such an argument is merely looking for an excuse to duck his responsibility—and is therefore making fools of the voters. Someone who really has the best interests of the public at heart will see at once that deregulation is necessary, and that the responsibility for enacting this must fall on the democratically elected legislators. It's time for Diet members to do their homework and assume their proper authority. They should do this by recognizing that, as members of the Diet, they are there to represent the people, and they should find the energy and the courage to do their job. I have no doubt that the people of Japan would prefer that kind of legislator.

As the process of deregulation moves ahead, the business community will also have an important role to play. For the good of the people, business ought to defy the bureaucrats. In the United States, those who brought about the deregulation of the long-distance telephone and airline industries were business people. In Japan as well, there are businesses—Honda Motor, Yamato Transport, MK Corporation (a Kyoto taxi company), among others—that stood up to the bureaucrats, battled tirelessly for deregulation, and then lowered their rates or started new enterprises. There are many cases where such actions ended in pluses for consumers and were advantageous for the businesses involved as well.

The fact that so many regulations exist in Japan tells us that there are just as many business opportunities waiting to be developed if the regulations were eliminated. Such new businesses are both important and valuable, and Japan's business people, too, should find the courage to rebuff the bureaucrats and strive for deregulation.

Many politicians, as well as company executives, are concerned only with preserving the status quo and protecting their own interests, and they are perfectly willing to hand over the affairs of the nation to the bureaucrats. This is exactly the ailment we must cure. The time has come to issue a declaration of independence from the ministries. We need to change Japan's standard operating procedure; instead of referring all issues to the bureaucrats, we should make the decisions ourselves, always keeping in mind the basic question, "What is best for the public?"

Toward a Genuine Democracy

In one sense, what Japan needs today is something it already has. The promise of democracy was bestowed upon Japan after World War II in the form of the new postwar Constitution. What it needs now is the fulfillment of that promise. The new Constitution set forth three branches of government centered on the legislature, in which representatives elected by the people were given the authority to govern. In form, Japan became a democracy like the free nations in North America and Europe. In fact, however, in the intervening years Japan's government has strayed far from that principle.

The guiding principle of our Constitution is the sovereignty of the people; in other words, democratic government, with the people in the driver's seat. This is set forth in the preamble: "Government is a sacred trust of the people, the authority for which is derived from the people, the powers of which are exercised by the representatives of the people, and the benefits of which are enjoyed by the people. This is a universal principle of mankind upon which this Constitution is founded."

But this "universal principle of mankind" has become an empty promise in Japan. As is well known, the three branches of government—the legislative, the judicial, and the administrative—have each become independent agents of supervision and control. The French philosopher Montesquieu, writing about Britain, said that each of the three branches of government there acts as a check on the other two. That is to say, when this tripartite balance is not maintained, the freedom of the people is endangered.

In Japan, on the other hand, the power of the bureaucrats

in the administrative branch to legislate is very real. After all, many Japanese bureaucrats retire from their ministries and become either Diet members, prefectural governors, or leaders of local organizations. This is evidence that the bureaucrats have accrued too much power, and this, in turn, skews the basic three-way balance of power and undermines the freedom of the people. Once this balance is lost, there is no way restore it.

There are people who claim that it was "Japanese-style democracy" that helped to make us into the economic giant we are, so this means that it is actually better than the democracy practiced in the West. Others insist that Japan has a unique place in history. But if we adopt these theories and turn away from the basic principle of democracy, Japan will eventually fail as a society.

Spreading the Spirit of Social Harmony Worldwide

The people of Japan have traditionally placed a high value on the concept of "*wa*," a word often translated as "social harmony" or "sense of community." In the first part of this book I explained how the development of a wet-rice agricultural society forced the people to place a high priority on harmony and cooperation within the community, and to this day this concept remains a powerful influence in Japanese culture.

Sometimes the importance of social harmony has even been invoked as an excuse for excessive control by the bureaucracy. The argument is that if Japan were deregulated, and real free market competition became the order of the day, people's great need to get along with others and work cooperatively would be lost. Thus, the ministries say, they must have the regulatory authority to preserve Japan's social traditions of mutual cooperation and assistance.

I, too, believe that social harmony is an admirable aspect of Japanese society, but I don't think this way of life should be confined to the narrow borders of the Japanese archipelago.

What we need to do now is abandon the old idea that only Japan can operate this way. It's time to spread the spirit of social harmony—and its concordant civility and social stability—around the world. The concept of a harmonious society can apply globally as well as locally. Indeed, I would say that this is our responsibility as members of global society, and I would like to see Japan communicate its marvelous concept of "*wa*" to other nations of the world.

MANAGEMENT FROM
THE HEART

Good Motives and Selfish Motives

As I explained in Chapter 2, a company must benefit the world and the public in order to succeed and grow. If management focuses only on pursuing the manager's own interests, even if the company is initially successful it will eventually lose the support of both the public and its employees. In other words, the company will eventually disappear.

At the end of 1958, I left the company I had been working for. I had been introduced to this company by a kind old professor of mine at university, and I had just started to make progress in my research there, so in a way I was sad to be leaving. However, there was a basic lack of trust between management and staff, and I was continually dissatisfied with the personnel department. At the age of twenty-seven, I finally plucked up the courage and quit. Seven of my friends, including some of my superiors, were kind enough to join me.

There then appeared on the scene a certain gentleman with whom I was not well acquainted but who offered to help this twenty-seven-year-old start his own company. And another gentleman put his house up as collateral for a ¥10 million bank loan to help found Kyocera. Taking into account the seven people who had left the company and bet their lives on me, I felt as if my back would break under the weight of all these people's expectations and the responsibility I felt toward them.

Although we had decided to start a company, having just quit our jobs and thereby lost our basic livelihood, we had no idea what would become of us. We were like a small ship set adrift upon a vast raging sea—without a compass. Throughout all this, the only people I could trust were my colleagues.

We realized that this mutual trust had to be preserved at all costs. With this resolve, the eight of us made a pledge in blood. If we had only banded together for the sake of selfish motives, even a blood pact would quickly have been broken, but we weren't like that. We had got together to realize a higher ideal. The pledge was as follows.

"We are not united for personal profit. We have no abilities, but we seek to work together to achieve something for the world and people in general. To this we friends do hereby commit ourselves."

In this way, before Kyocera was even founded, we established the goal of achieving "something for the world and people in general" by using my new ceramic technology. Our thoughts were, "We want to show our technology to the world. We want to repay our debts as fast as we can and put all our effort into building up the company as quickly as possible." We were full of youthful passion, because we were about to embark on an engineer's dream.

In this way, in 1959 my colleagues and I founded our company, later renamed Kyocera Corporation after our city, Kyoto, and our product, ceramics. Now we had a company, but we had neither capital nor equipment. The only thing we had, really, was our determination. I decided to base the company's management on this.

In reality, the human spirit is quite fickle, but if you look back through history, great things have been done by groups of friends bound by determination. There is no bond stronger than trust, and with this in mind we bet on the success of our company on the strength of our spiritual bond.

With a management based on this trust, Kyocera was somehow able to turn a profit after its first year. The following year, we hired eleven new technical school graduates and became a company of over sixty employees. It was at the end of that year that I had an experience that greatly changed my view of management.

These eleven new graduates, like us, worked hard until late at night each and every day. One day toward the end of the year, they came to me and said, "We've joined this new company and worked as you've asked us to, but we're worried. We don't know what will happen in the future, so we want you to guarantee us a certain pay raise each year. If you won't make that undertaking, we'll quit." Saying this, they thrust a sheet of written demands at me.

I was stunned by this development, so I took these employees to my tiny two-room home in a city housing project and talked with them continuously for three days and three nights.

"You ask for a promise," I told them, "but I can't give you one. We have just started this company, and I hired you to help us make it great. At this stage, not even I know what will happen. So how can I promise you a set salary in the future? All we can do is work hard each day and hope we succeed."

I tried my best to persuade them, but they still argued: "We understand your situation, but look at ours. We're scared about our futures. Are you sure this company will make it? If you could promise us a certain raise each year—then we could relax and get to work."

"What are you talking about?" I responded. "We're fighting to survive right now! If we were some huge company with a famous history, then I could easily promise you a raise next year and the year after that. But how can a one-year-old company make promises about what will happen a year from now—much less further ahead?

That ended the discussion. "That's the answer we expected," they said. "We quit."

There was nothing I could do, but I still felt miserable.

The Material and Spiritual Fulfillment of Employees
I am the second son of seven children, and my six siblings were still living with our parents in my hometown of Kagoshima. Being the second son, I was responsible for looking out for my siblings and parents and helping them survive in the tough postwar years. Since I was unable even to meet that obligation to my own family, how could I guarantee the future economic security of the employees I had hired?

I even thought, "I guess when you hire somebody, you accept the burden of looking after that person for the rest of his life. Starting a company was a mistake. I've begun something awful." Yet I had taken this step on my own responsibility, and there was no turning back.

I approached the new employees again, trying to convince them to stay. "I make no promises—except I'll do everything humanly possible to make this turn out well for you. Can't you trust me on that point? If you have the guts to quit, why don't you have the guts to stick with this company? Why don't you have the guts to trust me."

Finally I said, "Here's my proposal. Work for me and see if you think I'm taking advantage of you. If you think I'm playing you for fools, you can kill me."

Somehow, this appeal succeeded. They took back their written demands, stopped complaining, and went back to work, making the growth of Kyocera possible. They understood how serious I was, and that I was putting everything I had into this company.

From this experience I learned two important lessons. First, management means putting every ounce of your effort and ability into making your employees happy—whether you yourself like it or not. Second, every company must have a higher mission than simply increasing its executives' income. Until this confrontation, I had been managing the company with the aim of getting my technology out into the world, but I realized that this approach would not succeed. I became painfully aware of the need for a more direct management goal.

However, if you think only about the employees in your own company, you will end up thinking only about your company profits. Then you will not be able to fulfill your responsibility as a member of society. In addition to thinking about your employees, you need to think about how to contribute to society's progress. With this in mind, I adopted the following management motto for Kyocera: "Our goal is to strive toward both the material and the spiritual fulfillment of all employees in the Company, and through these serve mankind in its progress and prosperity."

After this, Kyocera continued to come up against indescribable difficulties, but because of our management motto, because management encouraged a spirit of mutual trust and honor, and because the employees put everything they had into their work, the company grew from a very small operation into the successful enterprise it is today.

The Challenge of the Telecommunications Industry
The first time Kyocera departed from its main field of business and entered a completely new one was with the foundation of Japan's second long-distance telephone company, DDI Corporation. This represented a new line of business in Japan, following the privatization and break-up of the telephone monopoly NTT, which was essentially Japan's version of the old Bell system of the United States.

Since I had been doing business in America for several years, I knew that communications costs there were far lower than in Japan. Both companies and individuals had various means available to communicate across the vast North American continent with almost no concern for the cost. On top of these low prices, American customers also received a variety of other services that were simply unthinkable in Japan at the time. This advanced development of the communications industry had immeasurable benefits both for industry and for people's daily lives.

Consequently, when the privatization of the telecommunications industry was finally approved in Japan, and new entries into the field of long-distance communications were permitted, I was sure that some of Japan's famous industrial giants would form a consortium to get into the business and provide lower nationwide long-distance telephone rates.

However, none of the big companies made any such effort, perhaps out of fear of the risks associated with competing against mighty NTT. Furthermore, even if an alliance of big firms did decide to engage in a high-risk battle with NTT, and even if they maximized the efficiency of their management, it was far from clear that they would succeed in lowering long-distance rates for the public. Moreover, there were further worries that, if such a consortium were formed, ultimately all it could do would be to obtain some telecommunications rights, which would not really benefit the public.

It was at this point that I began to wonder whether Kyocera—which was essentially a venture business—could take up this important industrial challenge. However, since our mission was to work to benefit the world and people in general, it seemed that we should get into the business of reducing long-distance telephone rates.

It was a scary prospect, to say the least. Kyocera was wary of head-on competition with NTT, whose sales at that time were well over ¥4 trillion (about US$40 billion) per year. Wouldn't we be just like Don Quixote tilting at a giant windmill? Anyway, it wasn't Kyocera's job to take on this kind of national project—we were a ceramics company, after all. Yet I couldn't rid myself of the idea that my people were the best suited to reducing long-distance telephone rates and making a contribution to the public good. I tossed these complicated and conflicting ideas around in my head for days on end with increasing frustration.

As I struggled with the issues, I began to argue with myself every night before I went to bed. Was my only motive in getting into the telecommunications business simply to lower long-distance telephone rates? I wanted to figure out if this really was my single unadulterated motive.

"Let's face it," I would say. "You're grandstanding. Your real goal is to become a figure of national prominence."

"No, that's wrong," I would answer. "My motive is to benefit the public, and I know our company can do it."

One month passed, and then another. Finally, I became convinced that my motives were good and not at all selfish. All my worries disappeared, and I decided to undertake the project, no matter how tough it might turn out to be. I could feel the courage surging inside me. I was confident that I really believed I was acting in accord with our corporate mission— and that assurance gave me further confidence. So I plunged ahead and started the company.

It was no small undertaking. To start the enterprise I needed an initial investment of at least US$1 billion—and if we failed, it would all be lost. However, the total savings of Kyocera since its foundation amounted to around US$1.5 billion, so even if it was a total disaster I knew that Kyocera would not be dragged down with it. After confirming this, I reviewed the plans with the board of directors, and after I explained that the most we could lose was US$1 billion, a consensus was reached to begin the enterprise.

Thus was decided our foray into the world of telecommunications, based on the simple idea of slightly lightening the burden on the general public as regards long-distance telephone rates. When I discussed the idea with my friends in the financial world—Akio Morita, chairman of Sony at that time; Jiro Ushio, chairman of Ushio Electronics; and Makoto Iida, chairman of Secom—they all immediately agreed with me and gladly offered their support. In this way, an early form of DDI was founded in 1984.

All did not go smoothly. As soon we went into the business, two other companies jumped into low-cost long-distance telecommunications, so the new age of the telephone business in Japan started with three companies. Of the three, DDI was reputed to be by far the most inferior.

After all, neither Kyocera nor I had any experience with telecommunications or its technology. Whereas the other two companies could just run cables along their train tracks or highways, DDI did not have those kinds of resources. We had to build a brand-new communications network from scratch— setting up parabola antennas on mountaintops and the like. On the financial side, we weren't backed by any powerful corporate group with affiliated firms and sub-contractors, so we had to build a network of agencies from scratch. Yet today DDI is sailing smoothly over the long-distance telecommunications seas, the front-runner in the group.

So how were we able to reverse our initial overwhelming disadvantage? Even today many people ask me this. My reply to them is: "The difference lay in our determination to do the job, because we got into this business through a sincere desire to give something to our customers."

Ever since DDI was founded, I have given pep talks to our employees: "You know, we have a once-in-a-lifetime chance here," I tell them repeatedly. "This is one way we can use our talents for something really meaningful—to give Japanese consumers better service at lower rates. A lot of people would love to have an opportunity like that, but not many get it. We should be thankful that we have the chance to perform this service for the public—so let's get to it!"

In this way, each employee under me at DDI came to share

in the simple belief that we were working for the public good. Every employee really wanted the company to succeed, and they began to put their all into their work. Seeing their dedication, the people in the administrative agencies began to support us as well. Even better, ordinary people sent letters of thanks and encouragement. In this way, we were able to gather a corps of dedicated people, and that is the key to the success of any enterprise.

Today, even with the stock market floundering, DDI has maintained its high price of about ¥8 million (US$80,000) per thousand shares since it was put on the market in 1993. The firm's total market worth is now valued at ¥1.9 trillion (US$19 billion).

Perhaps nobody will believe this, but when DDI went public, the founder did not own a single share, so I have made no capital gains from DDI's success. The companies that had kindly listened to my ideas and invested with me, however, received a large return and were delighted. I myself was quietly pleased as well. After all, a fairly simple idea had produced beneficial returns not only for our employees and the people of Japan but also for our investors.

Moving into Cellular Communications

Later, when we set up a cellular communications company to make portable and car phones as a subsidiary of DDI, everyone was betting against us. However, I was confident that founding a cellular communications company would benefit the general public just as much as the establishment of DDI had.

The day of portable telephones is definitely going to come. At present, whenever the phone rings in an office or home, you have to run to it to answer it. But soon the time will come when the phone will ring wherever you are, and you can call from wherever you are as cheaply as you like. You will be able to talk to anybody on the phone any time, any place. The day will undoubtedly come when the telephone is just such an ubiquitous device.

Indeed, one day a newborn baby will be assigned a telephone number even before his parents give him a name. The reason for this is miniaturization. Kyocera makes ceramic packages for large-scale integrated (LSI) circuits, so I knew how fast semiconductor technology was progressing, and I could see that in a few years the integrated circuits in a cellular phone—as well as the phone itself—would gradually become smaller and smaller, until soon you would be able to hold it in the palm of your hand. Just as I predicted, cellular phones, which were initially the size of a briefcase, are now small enough to fit in your pocket.

I was very confident, so I put my proposal to the board of directors of DDI. Among the directors are people from NTT and the Ministry of Posts and Telecommunications, who should understand the future of the communications industry better than anybody else, so I figured they would immediately raise their hands and support me. Instead, all they said was, "Mr. Chairman, please give it up."

"Why?" I asked.

"NTT's car phone project started five or six years ago and is still deeply in the red," they replied. "In America there are lots of car phone companies, but they're all in the red as well. No company in the world has succeeded in this. DDI has only just been set up, and nobody knows what the future will bring. Why would you want to risk your new company on a venture that is likely to fail?"

Among all of these "experts" only one young department chief agreed with me. So this department head and I decided to start a cellular communications company with just the two of us. Since there was another company applying to the Ministry of Posts and Telecommunications to enter the industry at the time, we wound up dividing the market into two geographical regions.

The problem lay in how to divide it. Since there were two companies, I proposed that we simply cut the Japanese archipelago into east and west zones, and draw straws to determine who would get what. The other firm, however, said that Tokyo was such a big market that they definitely wanted it; and since Nagoya was their home base, they couldn't give that up. The Ministry of Posts and Telecommunications forbade any sort of lottery, so reaching a conclusion was rather difficult. We finally agreed to give the Tokyo and Nagoya areas to our competitor—with DDI handling all the other areas.

When I returned to my company and reported to the board of directors, the majority judged that I had failed. "What a stupid agreement!" they upbraided me. "You gave up the most lucrative market! We're in big trouble now."

Of course, I had wanted to do business in Tokyo and Nagoya, where it is the easiest, but, on the other hand, if we didn't give those areas up, our whole cellular communications project might come to nothing at all. In this case I decided to take a step back and wrap up the talks. "No pain, no gain," the saying goes. Or, "In losing, we win."

That's what I told the board of directors, and we agreed to accept the less favorable market. Even so, we had to be thankful for the opportunity to start a cellular communications company. All we could do now was put all our efforts into making it a success.

One director was still unconvinced. "You gave away the icing!" he said. "You gave away all the icing, and all we get is the cake!"

"Exactly," I replied, "but nobody ever died from eating just cake. Let's all work together and turn that piece of cake into gold." It wasn't easy, but somehow I prevailed and convinced the board of directors to go ahead with the project.

All the employees knew that we were starting this enterprise under very unfavorable conditions. And we knew that, to make it work, everyone would have to give everything he had. Every employee maintained a firm resolve: "We cannot lose. We must succeed." Everyone worked his head off.

Once we actually started the company, our initial misgivings proved groundless. With DDI at the center, the eight companies of the cellular group (Kansai Cellular, Chugoku Cellular, Kyushu Cellular, Shikoku Cellular, Hokuriku Cellular, Tohoku Cellular, Hokkaido Cellular, and Okinawa Cellular) reported, in March 1996, sales of about ¥341.2 billion (US$3.4 billion) and profits of about ¥52.2 billion (US$52 million).

Chapter

8

Eleven Key Concepts for Effective Management

W hat is management? Books on management abound, and every year a sure-fire new management theory seems to be announced. But is management really that changeable? If managers vary their management systems every year tó fit the current trends, how can employees depend on them?

It is certainly worth being aware of market trends and management know-how, but there is also an actual skill called management, and that is something that has to be learned. Neglecting this skill can result in business failure, and I firmly believe there are certain principles that a manager in any age should always keep in mind. You could call them the overriding "Key Concepts of Effective Management." I would now like to discuss them one by one.

1. Establish Clear Goals

"Why am I doing what I'm doing right now?" It is essential to establish a clear objective that answers this question, such as "To realize my dreams," or "To improve life for my employees," or maybe even "To make money." Obviously, different people have different objectives, but are the objectives crystal clear? Clear goals are the first thing a business manager should establish.

In setting one's goals, it is essential to aim high. For example, suppose a manager who has until now been fairly poor decides that he wants to make his business succeed and earn a lot of money so that he can enjoy living in a big house with his family. In other words, he sets the aim of making money as his principle purpose in business. If he works hard he can attain his objective.

However, once he achieves it—and he is indeed living happily in a large house with his family—he grows contented. He celebrates having attained his goal and stops working hard. He begins to enjoy the pleasures of life and loses all interest in management. After some time his business falls apart. Why? Because his objectives in running the business were too limited. Making money is a fine objective for a business, but you need to aim high—make your goal the largest sum of money you can imagine.

Another important factor is making your goal as just, as fair, and as honorable as possible. If a manager makes personal profit the sole rationale for running a business, he won't be able to motivate his employees, however few he may have. No employee wants to sacrifice himself to work for the private gain of the manager. So the target in running a business needs to be fair, just, and ambitious. It must be something that all company's employees—the factory workers, the salesmen who deal directly with the customers, the researchers who develop products—can believe in sincerely, something that even their families may be proud of.

Taking my own company as an example, in the second year after Kyocera was incorporated it adopted as its philosophy: "Our goal is to strive toward both the material and the spiritual fulfillment of all employees in the company, and through these serve mankind in its progress and prosperity."

The founding principle of DDI Corporation, our long-distance telephone company, was: "To provide the people of Japan with the cheapest possible long-distance communication service." Whenever I have a chance, I remind employees of this goal, making it an objective we can all share.

Goals are crucial for any company. Keep the objective as large and as multifaceted as possible. It must moreover be something that every member of the company can believe in, so that it can become everyone's goal. In this way the company will become a unified whole centered around its managers, and will evolve into a powerful productive group.

2. Establish Specific Targets

By "target" I mean a numerical goal for the company to aim for. It is a specific objective, such as, so many years from now we want our sales to be this much and our profits to be this high. A manager must have this kind of clear, specific target.

Furthermore, the manager must make this target his own personal target and must want to attain it with his whole heart. He must continually, daily, remind himself and all his employees of the target as something that must definitely be reached, and he must hold it as the company's dream for the future.

In 1959, Kyocera (then called Kyoto Ceramic) started out by renting part of a wooden warehouse from another company in the Hara neighborhood, in the West Ward of Kyoto's Central District. That was our first factory. I used to tell our young workers: "First, we will become the biggest company in Hara. When we're the biggest in Hara, we will become the biggest in the West Ward. When we're the biggest in the West Ward, our next goal is to become the biggest in the Central District. To be the biggest company in Central would make us a huge company. That would be phenomenal."

At the time, none of this seemed possible. Even so, I repeatedly said, "Someday we'll definitely be the biggest company in all Kyoto. Once we're the biggest in Kyoto, we'll become the biggest ceramics company in Japan. After we've become the biggest in Japan, we'll become the biggest in the world."

We aimed high, to put it mildly. We said, "This is our target—no matter what." And we never let our hopes flag. In the course of time, we actually did achieve each of these goals that I had continually reminded my employees of.

I'll explain this in more detail in the next chapter, but things that you really wish for are the things you always get. Whenever something doesn't come to you, it's because you didn't want it enough—or you didn't keep trying. First you must set a target—and then you have to do whatever it takes to attain that target. These are the essential elements of any successful business.

3. Work Harder Than Anybody Else

"Work steadily, one step at a time, on the basic business; maintain unceasing diligence."

Once you have determined the objectives of your enterprise and set your targets, it is essential to work harder than anybody else to achieve them. All great things start from plain diligence, working one step at a time and repeating this again and again. It is essential to work steadily on the basic business and to be unswervingly diligent. You might doubt this and ask how working diligently and sticking to the business at hand could affect distant goals. Yet all great things are only achieved by taking one small step at a time and doing this over and over again.

Although many of you might think this is obvious, few people can actually achieve it. Everybody works hard to some extent, but working harder than anybody else is a completely different matter. You might think you are working diligently— so hard that you couldn't work any harder—but if you look around there's always somebody working harder than you. Some people say they are naturally talented and their work is more efficient, so they do not need not to work as hard as others. However, nothing great ever came from mere talent and efficiency. What it takes is real work.

Some people compliment me for my foresight and others say I am an excellent manager, but they're all wrong. Good market sense and foresight are nothing but the results of putting every last ounce of your energy into your work. Because you are enthusiastic, because you are diligent, you notice things that other people don't even think about.

They say there's no genius that can defeat hard work—and this is absolutely right. Nobody is so much more gifted than any other person, but some people work a lot harder than others. And this difference—that is, more input—ultimately results in an even bigger difference—that is, much more output.

4. Keep Sales at a Maximum and Expenses to a Minimum

> *"Count what comes in, and control what goes out. Don't seek profit; that will come later."*

The way to make a business succeed is to keep sales at a maximum and expenses to a minimum. Maximizing sales requires clever and original ideas. Minimizing expenses also requires clever and original ideas. Putting this concept into practice is the acid test for managers.

Most managers don't see it this way. They only seek profit. Their reasoning runs roughly like this: "Most companies in my industry make about X percent profit, so I'll aim for that, too." Once a manager settles into that rut, originality goes out the window. In fact, good management isn't about trying to make a certain amount of profit. Profit is simply the result of maximizing sales and minimizing expenses. "Count what comes in, and control what goes out" is a fundamental tenet of management, and it is far more important than "make X percent profit."

To "count what comes in" and keep it at a maximum, and to really "control what goes out" and keep it at a minimum, takes hard work and strong ambition. And this passionate ambition makes you think up the clever and original ideas you need to achieve it.

Something that you don't see too often in Japan any more are the noodle vendors who used to set up their stalls in the street at night and sell noodles. I used to eat at these stalls whenever I was working late, and I also used the noodle vendors as a model for the employees at my high-tech business.

Although all these vendors only sell noodles in broth, this seemingly simple business can be run in an almost infinite number of ways. What comes in is flour, soup stock, fish paste, onions, and some other ingredients. To minimize the outlay on these ingredients, you can come up with innovative ideas about where to buy them and how much to stock, what ingredients to use for the soup, and so on. And to maximize sales you can come up with all sorts of original ideas about how much to charge, where and when to set up your stall every night, and so on.

How should you actually purchase the ingredients? How should you actually sell the noodles? It is here that you can judge how innovative and clever a vendor really is. The difference in expenses between two vendors with different purchasing strategies and the difference in sales between two vendors with different sales approaches might seem insignificant on a day-to-day basis, but over the course of a year these differences can add up to a vast disparity. Some vendors manage to make a fortune in a few years, and some will still only have one stall after several decades.

As we may see from this example, no matter how small one's business is, good management aimed at maximizing sales and minimizing expenses will eventually result in big profits, and after several years it will make the difference between a growing business and failure or stagnation.

5. Pricing is the Heart of Management

Many managers feel that their duties should consist of approving new projects and making decisions on sales strategies, and that they should delegate decisions on product pricing to their subordinates. If the manager then complains to his underlings about profits and sales not increasing, one can only say that he knows absolutely nothing about management. This is because sales and profits are heavily dependent on pricing decisions. These are extremely serious matters for which managers should be responsible.

Products whose prices are determined by the competition—for example, in the case of a product made by four or five competing companies—do not need pricing decisions. In such cases, there is no choice but to go with the market price and work hard to keep sales at a maximum and expenses at a minimum, as described above.

However, for products with little competition—like the noodles sold by the street vendors mentioned earlier—prices can be freely chosen. The price of a bowl of noodles is really up to the vendor. In reality, if one vendor sells for ¥300, another vendor may be selling the same kind of noodles in the same area for ¥500. The higher you set the price, the more profit you make per bowl, but the fewer bowls you can sell. On the other hand, the lower you set the price, the more bowls you will sell, but the profit you will make on each bowl sold will be less.

In this way, sales and profits depend heavily on the price per bowl of noodles, so the most prosperous vendor is always the one who chooses the highest price he knows his customers will pay and still be satisfied with the value they receive. In other words, he is the one who has found, among all profitable prices, the price that generates the most sales.

I have used the simple example of noodle vendors, but the

importance of pricing decisions is the same for any product. A manager must find the price, among all profit-producing prices, that his customers will be glad to pay for the product. This is an important duty of the manager. For every company that lowered its prices too much, failed to make any profit, and went bankrupt, there is a company that ignored the market and kept its prices high until the warehouse was full of unsold goods. All such tragedies are caused by bad pricing decisions.

In this way, pricing decisions are the basis of management. A company can only develop when the correct price has been assigned to each of its products. A price decision is not something a manager can delegate. A good manager must think seriously about pricing and take on this important responsibility himself.

6. Do Not Be Afraid to Dream

"Have unlimited dreams so strong that they penetrate your subconscious."

The workings of the human mind are delicate and complex. We normally accept that the thoughts in our mind are only the ones we are conscious of, but this is not the case. The human mind is always working on a deeper level, even on things we are not conscious of; this happens in what is called the subconscious.

When we have an ambition, so many obstacles may stand in the way that it may seem almost impossible to attain. Yet despite this, we may still have a strong desire to achieve it. If this desire were taken away, we would be left with just a lazy daydream—"Gee, if only I could..."—which will never result in anything. The passionate desire I'm talking about gives us visions of ways to realize our dreams, and it is this kind of desire that can penetrate our subconscious.

For it to do this, we must think of nothing but our dream, day and night, asleep or awake. If we have something we wish to succeed in, we must think about it twenty-four hours a day. Then we will be thinking of the ideas we need to achieve that ambition twenty-four hours a day, and before we know it we will be moving toward its realization.

7. A Manager Must Be a Fighter

Like the lord of a medieval castle, a manager must be willing to take on all comers—and be assured of victory each time. A manager leads his employees with the same intense fighting spirit as a feudal warrior.

Once a manager has decided what he wants, he must have the strength of will to achieve it, no matter what. One condition for maintaining that willpower is good health—strong muscles—but the fundamental condition is his competitive drive: "We will not lose. We will not retreat." Without a strong confrontational spirit, a manager can never hope to win out in competition and expand his business.

Management is a serious daily battle of win or lose. A manager does not always receive good news. More often it is bad: "It looks like we're going to lose that order," or "It looks like we're going to lose this fight." No matter how adverse the conditions he is placed in, a manager must keep his will to win alive: "Come what may, we will not lose." Seeing this, his subordinates will become motivated, since his competitive drive will be infectious.

On the other hand, if the leader should display even a touch of weakness, that, too, is infectious. It will instantly spread and destroy morale throughout the company. Once a company's morale has fallen, it is nearly impossible to resurrect it, and subsequently, the firm itself will begin to deteriorate. To succeed in the face of brutal competition requires both a strong determination and the competitive drive to maintain it.

8. Be Sincere and Generous

"Have partners in business. Enjoy the work.
And make sure everybody has fun."

The intense will to compete—a competitive drive stronger than that of any challenger—is necessary, but this is in itself not sufficient for success. It must be accompanied by kindness. The greater a manager's competitive drive, the greater the kindness he must have in his heart.

In doing business, people must have partners, for nobody can make his profits rise by himself. The basic rule of any business is: the buyers must be happy and the sellers must be happy. The kind of thinking that is centered on profit for yourself without any regard for your partners may achieve temporary success, but it won't provide longtime prosperity. Management isn't a zero-sum proposition or a win–lose game. In addition to striving for success, you need to be decent to everyone you work with—including your customers and your employees.

I believe a manager must have the competitive drive and must work with unrivaled zeal and energy. However, being strong in these areas alone is inadequate. The novelist Raymond Chandler got it precisely right, I believe, when he wrote, "If I wasn't hard, I wouldn't be alive. If I couldn't ever be gentle, I wouldn't deserve to be alive." Nobody will be impressed with a manager who is merely strong. A manager who is kind and strong at the same time will be infinitely more attractive as a personality and will be loved by all.

9. Look Ahead with Cheerful Confidence

"Life turns out the way you plan it in your heart."

A successful manager, in addition to having the qualities of being intensely ambitious and tremendously competitive, must also have a cheerful disposition. He cannot be constantly critical or negative. A gloomy face must be avoided at all costs, and any behavior that makes employees feel dissatisfied or unfairly treated is unacceptable. To be successful, a manager has to look ahead to the future with a cheerful confidence. You have to keep your dreams alive in your heart and maintain a positive and accepting attitude no matter what comes up.

In times of recession, or when bad business performance persists for a few years, many people worry themselves sick with negative thoughts: "At this rate we're heading for bankruptcy." And sure enough, people who are obsessively pessimistic invite negative things to happen to them. Real life mirrors the thoughts you hold within you. No matter how bad the situation may get, you cannot let it sour you. With a confident eye turned to the future, you must believe that, no matter what, nothing can go permanently wrong. You have to plug away at life and work cheerfully.

10. Good Management Takes Guts

"Cowardly behavior is untenable."

To make decisions that uphold these fundamental principles takes a lot of courage, for the correct decisions will not always be welcomed by everyone. People may criticize you for them and make your life difficult. You may even be disliked. Thus, making the correct decisions in the face of possible unpleasantness takes real courage.

When the top man loses the courage to make the right decisions and begins to flounder, there is no way to conceal this from his subordinates. They will spot it right away. Even the slightest sign of cowardice will upset the relationship of trust between a manager and his employees. The subordinates of a cowardly leader will begin to accept such behavior and the ethics of the group will quickly decline. Then the right decisions will not be made, and compromise will become the norm. Indeed, compromise will become the way to get on in the world and will become the rationale of life. Then the core abilities of the company will atrophy.

However, to say that courage is essential is not to endorse managers who jump in impulsively and make foolish decisions simply for the sake of appearing to be brave. Management cannot be rash; instead it must depend on a series of serious and carefully considered decisions. A manager, in addition to courage, must also have a cautiousness that results from a certain sort of patience.

It is hard to be courageous and careful at the same time. I feel that a man who is cautious and timid by nature and has been forced by necessity to develop courage is more appropriate as a leader than someone with the spirit of a caveman. The only way to become brave is to accumulate a range of experiences and train oneself to be bold. When a careful, cautious person has such experiences and builds up his courage, this is true courage. A manager must develop this kind of courage and apply it to his work.

11. Be Original and Have Creative Ideas

> *"Continue, without pause, to improve tomorrow more than today, and the next day more than that. Have creative and original ideas every day."*

Original work does not refer only to difficult tasks such as developing high-level technology. It is about continually improving your workplace through innovative ideas, making it a better place tomorrow than it was today, and making it even better the following day. Each person must get into the habit of thinking, "What can I, in my place, do to correct yesterday's errors and work more efficiently than yesterday?"

Although a high level of education is considered an advantage, a person who lacks this sort of education cannot be said to be unable to do original work. Genuine originality is not related to education or innate ability. It comes instead from constantly thinking innovatively, from never being satisfied with the current situation, and from constantly working, even unknown to everybody else, to improve things.

Kyocera started out making electrical components and moved on to include every field of ceramics applications—mechanical components, medical materials, decorative products, and so on—and also expanded its business to electronic devices, optical devices, and information and communication technology. In the beginning, we were far from large—nor did we have all the technology. Rather, we built the company by starting with the technology we had and applying it to other fields, continuing to expand as we did so.

The Way of the Manager

"What is so important about the human spirit?"
you may ask. The answer is that in business,
as in every other area of life, the way you
look at things and the workings of the human spirit play deci-
sive roles. The secret of success in both life and business is
found in the human spirit. Success awaits those who aim high
and dream big. Those who are satisfied with small dreams,
who are content with lazy compromises, can only hope to live
small and lazy lives.

What kind of attitude, what sort of spirit, leads to success?
The essential philosophy lies within the ideals I refer to as
"love," "sincerity," and "harmony." I'll explain these more
fully in the next chapter, but these ideals exist on the highest
spiritual level. The ability to make other people's happiness
your own happiness is "love"; focusing on ideals that will benefit the world and its people is "sincerity"; and the hope that
not just yourself, but all those around you, can live in a constant state of happiness is "harmony." This philosophy contains the basic foundation of success.

You might write off these ideas as the ruminations of a

hopeless idealist. Not so. I'm no saint, and I can't always achieve the three ideals I have outlined. However, my measure of success has been due to hard work and my efforts to maintain this humanistic philosophy.

When conveying these concepts to my employees, I call them the "Kyocera Philosophy." One of the reasons I started DDI was to prove to my employees that if you have a pure and humane outlook, you can succeed in any venture. This kind of philosophy is important for the whole human race, for the human spirit is the same whether in the East or the West. Kyocera has 14,000 employees overseas—about as many as in Japan—but I explain the Kyocera Philosophy to them all in the same way.

Once I gave a talk about the essence of this Kyocera Philosophy in front of my American employees and colleagues. At the time I was a little apprehensive about how they would react: "I can try to explain these Japanese concepts," I thought, "but they may just laugh at me. They'll decide that the chairman is some kind of religious nut, and their confidence in the company will be affected."

However, when I actually gave my speech, I got a huge response. At the cocktail party afterwards, many people—both men and women—came up to shake my hand and say, "That was a really excellent speech."

I realized then that in the United States, where individualism is so prevalent, people occasionally end up feeling deeply isolated. I assume the reason Americans have such lively parties in their homes (which is unusual among the Japanese, who rarely entertain at home) is to find some way of communicating with others. Many people have problems—but can find nobody to talk about them with. Perhaps for this reason lot of people seek counseling from psychiatrists. However, there are also many Americans who go to a church or temple every week. In this sense, Americans have a better understanding than the Japanese when it comes to the importance of the spiri-

tual dimension for the individual and for society as a whole.

Americans show a strong interest in spiritual matters, and when talk turns to such matters, even if with a purely Eastern philosophical approach, they show very great willingness to listen. After my speech, for example, people said, "We understand the notion of a spiritual dimension in management. And we can trust a manager who is open about his spiritual ideas."

Whenever I talk about the importance of a kind and considerate attitude, of the correct and pure spirit a person should have, people become really interested. This is true both in Japan and overseas, and in this way spiritual bonds are made.

On my visits to Kyocera's overseas factories, I frequently talk to the employees about the Kyocera Philosophy. A few years ago, when I was having a conversation at one factory in the United States, an employee said, "The kind of thing you're always talking about could be put in a drawing like this." Then he drew a sketch that did, indeed, perfectly illustrate what I'm always talking about.

As you can see in this drawing (page 130), the balloon bears Kyocera's corporate motto, "Respect the Divine and Love People," and the words which embody the corresponding philosophy—"Sincerity," "Love," and "Harmony"—and it has uplifted many of our employees. Our corporate motto, "Pursue material and spiritual happiness and the welfare of mankind," can lead us confidently into the future.

What this drawing expresses is that the correct human spirit and attitude can lift up our weightiest ideals (in this case, our management motto) and make them soar to a world of happiness in the sky. In other words, the drawing quite accurately expresses what I always say: "Spirit and philosophy are the driving forces behind all great things. For this reason we must study the human spirit." When I saw this drawing, I felt without question that it had, indeed, been worth my while to explain the Kyocera Philosophy overseas—and I was delighted.

The Way of the Leader

There are certain qualities that are essential in a leader. First, he must pay careful attention to his physical health. If he is in poor health when he is making decisions, the human instinct for self-protection may influence his criteria, and the resulting decisions may be the wrong ones. To take the argument to its extreme, a leader who no longer cares about preserving his health and strength has reached the point where he should step down. A leader must be equipped with good health and a strong will to allow him to make decisions free of self-interest.

Furthermore, a leader must have a perpetual curiosity. Unless a leader is constantly searching for something new, constantly thinking up original ideas, and constantly introducing innovations, the group cannot hope to continue to progress or develop. If a leader settles for preserving the status quo, then that kind of mindset, which seeks only security, will permeate the entire group.

Moreover, a leader must be able to give his subordinates clear objectives, and he must personally believe that those objectives can be achieved. He must be able to show his subordinates step by step how this can be done and convince them that the targets can really be attained.

Incidentally, a person who has the credentials of a leader—the ability to get things accomplished, the power to control people, strength of character—needs to think deeply about the reason he was given such talents. You could argue that leadership skill is a resource that is distributed at a certain rate by fate in order that groups of people can be led to happiness. If this is the case, a person who chances to be given such skills should use them for the benefit of other people. Such a leader has no right to turn a God-given talent into his personal property and use it for himself alone. He should be modest at heart. He must possess no self-interest, and he must have the courage to work for the welfare of the group, even at the cost of personal sacrifice.

When a leader sets up an office, he must not put himself first and design an office that is easy for himself to work in, but rather an office that is easy for the majority of his employees to work in. If a leader wants a workplace that is only comfortable and convenient for himself, none of his subordinates will respect him. If he puts his subordinates first and sacrifices his own interests to make a workplace that feels good to them, then his subordinates will be excited and he will win their trust and respect. In other words, the harmony, order, and success of the workplace will be ensured.

Obviously, work is not something a leader does alone. Unless subordinates work with the same passion as their leader, the business will not succeed. If a leader can share his dreams with his subordinates and then raise their morale to his own level, the business will succeed no matter what happens. In so doing, he will raise his subordinates' energy level to be equal to or greater than his own. If he can raise their energy to the point where they don't know whether they are working for the business or for themselves, then he is already 90 percent successful.

Furthermore, a leader cannot in any way be a coward. He must make his orders clear. If they turn out to be wrong, he must admit his error clearly, with no excuses. The leader of a group must not only understand the rules and morals of the group, but he must also live by them. If he himself practices what he preaches, others will naturally follow him.

Subordinates keep a keen eye on their leader's every move. If he acts like a coward, his subordinates will know right away, and he will instantly lose the trust and respect of his subordinates. This will lead to a decline in the morale of the group as the leader's actions, attitude, and image spread like wildfire. The group is a mirror that reflects its leader.

Thus, a leader must be strict with himself and yet deal lovingly with his subordinates. This love cannot be indulgent. A child may be spoilt because everyone thinks he is cute, but through this his development may be hindered and his life messed up. On the other hand, it is also possible to raise a child too strictly, with too much discipline, and ruin a great life. Dealing with your subordinates is not dissimilar.

If a leader does not show any commitment and simply flatters his subordinates, he may get a reputation for kindness, but that will not really help the younger people. Flattery makes young people happy at first, but eventually it spoils them. In the long run, employees will receive better training and will mature better as human beings under a strict leader.

To be loved by his subordinates and to be able to train and educate them, a leader must have outstanding human qualities. The title of "president" or "director" may buy politeness from employees, but it cannot buy their respect. The most important thing for a leader is to be trusted and respected. Thus, in addition to thinking hard about "What does it mean to be a human being?" and "How should I live?" a leader must earnestly pursue the question, "How can I improve my human qualities?" When he can improve his character in this way, he will become a true leader.

These are what I consider to be the qualities of a leader. Finally, I must mention a few things I always say to the presidents of companies we do business with. These are people who understand the points I've made so far in this chapter. As the top men in their companies, they should pay particular attention to the following thoughts. I would be happy if all people in such positions or seeking such positions use them as a reference.

1) When I founded DDI, I asked myself, "Are your motives for doing this selfish, or do you have a more legitimate reason?" And from those days on I worked hard to be fair and just, to have courage, to hold to the notion of "Respect the divine and love people." This mindset shaped the establishment of DDI and led to its current success.

2) Efficient management means eliminating waste and excess.

3) Manage your business to provide products and services that the general public and your customers will appreciate, and aim for a highly profitable company.

4) While pursuing the material and spiritual happiness of all employees, work to contribute to the advancement and development of society as a whole and to provide your stockholders with a good return on their investment.

5) Avoid the inflexibility and hierarchy typical of the bureaucracy and large companies; aim for a flexible and optimistic organization.

6) Be impartial in personnel decisions and aim for fairness; personal bias must never be tolerated.

7) Avoid independent decision-making; make decisions as a group, in a democratic manner.

8) Don't make decisions based on habit, conventional wisdom, or the way things have customarily been done. Always remember to ask the question: "What is the correct thing for a human being to do?" All decisions should be made in accordance with this principle.

PART

4

MY THEORY OF HUMANITY

Chapter 10

Fate and Human Will

W hen I was a child, I was very mischievous, the king of troublemakers. I didn't study too much in school, and I was always taking a group of kids off somewhere to play. From playing with those kids, I feel that I learned a lot about what it means to be a human being.

A child is pure in heart and observes his leader with a sharp eye. If he detects any cowardly behavior or feels that he is no longer being looked after, he will quickly break away. No matter how strong an opponent I faced in a fight, I had to stand firm and deal with him. I also had to share my snacks with my friends. Otherwise, the kids who were my protégés would immediately begin looking elsewhere for a leader. At some point in my youth I learned the fickleness of people and what you have to do to keep somebody's loyalty. This experience was a lot more useful in later life than my school studies.

At the beginning of 1945, when I was thirteen, I got tuberculosis. As my grandmother and grandfather had just died of the same disease, my family developed the uneasy feeling that it was cursed with tuberculosis. At that time, you may remember, it was incurable, and with the war going on we couldn't get enough nutritious foods, so I feared that I would soon die.

During this period, one of the women in the neighborhood brought to my bed the complete edition of Masaharu Taniguchi's *The Truth of Life*. She said, "This book contains some helpful things, so read it all the way through, even if you don't understand everything." Beset by anxiety as I was, each word and phrase of this book struck me with their freshness, and a feeling that might even be called religious began to stir deep inside me.

The following are some passages from that book that still impress me even today:

> It is a mistake to think of suffering as unhappiness. Those who understand how essential suffering is to the growth of the spirit are joyful even in suffering.

> People's attitude toward sickness, i.e., that such and such is unsanitary, or that if you do this you will get sick, is misguided. People get sick because they believe that "disease" exists, and they become obsessed with disease and with their attempts to avoid it.

> When people say they "suffered a disaster," they think this means that disaster—some violent outside force—came and struck them down, even though they had done nothing wrong. The real reason a person suffers a setback is because in his pessimistic heart he is expecting one. Disaster will always find such a person. Not one thing in this world will come to you unless your heart invites it in.

> Strong belief and a clear vision will control your fate. What happens to you is a direct result of your belief and your vision.

> To achieve your heart's desire, you must think about it

non-stop; you must patiently maintain your ambition and your dedication to it.

As I read this book, I began to think that the reason I had caught tuberculosis was because my heart had invited it. Then, one day, toward the end of the war, I found I had been cured. This experience gave me a chance to think seriously about the human spirit and how life depends on it.

Later, I experienced repeated setbacks and frustration with exams and suchlike, but, as I have explained before, I eventually managed to found Kyocera in 1959. The rest is history. Since then, even while totally dedicated to my work, as both a manager and an engineer I have constantly thought about the spiritual dimension that my employees and I should have.

In this sense I feel that most managers today react only to external phenomena—the "bubble economy" of the late 1980s, the recession of the early 1990s, and so on—and don't realize that they are ignoring the most important element of management—the human spirit. They spend all their energy developing strategies for pursuing their own interests and never even try to grapple with the real problem of management—the human heart.

The most important management resource is people, which is why it is crucial, especially in these times, to find the best aspects of the human spirit.

Strong Willpower

Just as a company cannot develop without making new products, human beings cannot grow without taking on new challenges and, through that, making new discoveries. To do this a strong determination is necessary.

In our society we already have a high degree of law and order. For most people, living in accordance with this established social order is the pleasantest way to live and the one that causes the least friction. In contrast, it is much harder not to depend on the established order but to blaze a new trail. For this reason, most people unconsciously choose to live a normal, sensible life, without ever trying to take on new challenges. The most demanding—and most rewarding—challenge is to undertake a task that other people could not handle. It is from this tough challenge that we achieve real growth.

In taking up a challenge that conventional wisdom holds to be impossible, the first requirement is courage and a strong will. Even if you possess these qualities and accept the toughest challenge to create something new, your task will not be complete. You need to believe your creation is a good thing and will definitely help society, so your next challenge is to gain general acceptance for your innovation.

This may sound easy, but it is not. Most people function in accordance with the status quo and are hesitant when it comes to accepting something new. The more revolutionary something is, the more it will be criticized and attacked from all sides. This situation must be overcome. If you create something new, you may gain some personal satisfaction, but this will not be sufficient if you fail to win wider acceptance of the idea. At this point what is most essential is unshakable confidence and a strong conviction that your achievement will definitely contribute to the advancement of society. By keeping up your efforts and your determination, you will eventually be accepted by the public, and you will finally have achieved something.

In summary, when you accept the challenge of achieving something new, the most important factor is to maintain a strong determination to prevail. Only when you have this willpower will you achieve anything. When you challenge the apparently impossible and set out to attain it, the strength of your willpower will greatly affect the results. As we try to make something new under unfavorable conditions, our strongest asset is the greatest weapon any man can possess: the human spirit.

In Buddhist philosophy, when something we conceive of in our minds happens in the real world, it is said that "the nature of your thoughts creates karma." You have a thought, and the action that results from the thought reflects the nature of the thought. Thoughts are the "wavelengths" of the spirit, and as such can be considered a form of energy. When you maintain a strong determination, energy starts condensing and showing up around us, a phenomenon described by the above dictum.

We can understand how true this saying is just by looking closely at the phenomena around us. The physical world appears in the way we conceive it in our mind. On the small scale it's our family, friends, and company; on the large scale, it is the nation and indeed the entire earth: they are all reflections of the images we hold in our minds.

Fate is Affected by Good Thoughts

Every human being has a destiny, which is different from human will. Our fate is decided by what in Buddhist philosophy is called "*innen*," a term that means roughly "cosmic connections." These connections have a great influence over what happens to us—in other words, they are the "karma" resulting from the previous history of your soul. So to turn your fate in a good direction, you have to create good karma in your present life. The dictum that I just mentioned, "The nature of your thoughts creates karma," means that your fate can change depending on whether you think good or bad thoughts. What you think creates karma, and karma decides your fate.

People occasionally get into unexpected trouble. This might be considered a disaster resulting from the accumulated karma your soul is burdened with. Indeed, your subsequent lives in the future depend heavily on what you thought and what was in your heart when you encountered such trouble. When you stumble in life—when you get sick, or have an accident, for example—you should not take it in a negative way but, instead, you should make an effort to interpret it in a positive light.

Each disaster you encounter can help to erase your old karma, so when you have a setback, you should be grateful. View it positively: "It's a good thing this setback was so serious." By interpreting even disasters in a positive light, you can change your fate for the better. If you are perpetually cheerful and maintain a consistently positive outlook, your fate will definitely change for the better.

One Chinese classic I often talk about is *Yun Chih Lu* (in Japanese, *Inshitsuroku*), written by Yuan Liao-fan during the Ming dynasty (1368–1644).

When Liao-fan was young, he once met an aged traveler at a neighborhood temple. The traveler was skilled at fortune-telling, and he told Liao-fan, "I received a command from heaven to teach you law, and I came all the way from the south to find you." Though it seemed a strange story, the boy invited the old man to his home, asked his mother to cook him supper, and let him spend the night.

At that time, to become a government administrator or minister in China, one had to pass the civil service exam. The old man predicted to Liao-fan that, "In the future, you will take the civil service exam. First you'll take practice exams; in the first practice exam, you'll come fourteenth; in the second, you'll come seventy-second; and in the final practice exam you'll come ninth. Then you'll get an appointment from the local official until you take the actual exam. You'll also get married, but unfortunately you will not have any children. You'll die of old age on August 24, in your fifty-third year."

Liao-fan was still young, so when he heard the old man's predictions he thought, "This is impossible!" However, his life followed the predictions exactly. As it turned out, however, he was directed to take the actual exam a year earlier than the old man had foreseen, so he thought, "Well, he was a little out on this." Yet just before he was to take the test, the administrator came up to him and said, "I can't allow this person to take the test," so he didn't get to take the exam that year after all.

The next year, however, a different administrator read an essay written by Liao-fan and let him pass without even taking the exam, saying, "Nobody else could write such an excellent essay." Everything was unfolding just as the old man had predicted.

At that point Liao-fan began to ponder: "Life is a profound mystery. Even before I was born, my entire fate was determined." Until then Liao-fan had been a dedicated student and a hard worker, but now he figured that if his fate had already been completely determined, there was no need to work hard or worry about anything. He was misled by his understanding of fate.

After Liao-fan passed the exam, he went to stay for a while in Nanjing, where he visited a famous elder at a Zen temple and did zazen—intense, silent meditation—for three days. The elder observed Liao-fan's zazen style and praised him. "This is excellent! You clearly have no worldly thoughts or distractions. Your heart has not one cloud in it. Congratulations on having achieved nirvana despite your youth."

Liao-fan replied, "No, I have not achieved nirvana," and he proceeded to explain his situation to the elder. "Actually, when I was a boy, I met an old traveler who foretold my entire life, and since then everything has happened just as he predicted. I can't have children, and I will die when I am fifty-three. So I have nothing to worry about. I just have to live out the rest of my life."

As soon as he heard this, the elder was furious. "I thought you were a wise man, but you are a fool!" And he went on to explain something important. "Fate is decided by your previous karma before you were born. But after you're born into this world, what you hold in your heart affects the karma that will determine your future."

In China, people believe that fate can be changed. To alter

the force called "fate" requires a counterforce called "human will." You can change your fate in a positive way by thinking good thoughts. In other words, if you have enough kindness to make others' happiness your own happiness, your fate will be changed for the better.

Many people think that "good thoughts" means charity. Some say, "Well, I'd like to help people, but I don't have any money, so I can't." But this is wrong. "Good thoughts" means empathy. It means having the generosity of spirit to rejoice at other people's happiness and to feel sad at other people's sorrow.

There's a saying that goes, "The family that does good deeds is a happy family." This just means that if a family accumulates a lot of good deeds, good things will befall its children and grandchildren. As the elder explained to Liao-fan, "If you accumulate goodness, your fate will change for the better."

Liao-fan was convinced by the priest. He went home and said to his wife, "Evidently, thinking good thoughts can change our fate for the better. Let's try to make our hearts more beautiful, little by little. Let's see which one of us can think more often how much we hope people will be happy." They did this conscientiously, and soon a child was born to the childless couple.

When Liao-fan's child was grown up, he said to him, "Even though you weren't supposed to be born, you've grown into a fine young man, and now it is time for you to go out into the world. Even though I was fated to die at fifty-three, I am now sixty-nine. After I listened to the priest's words years ago, my fate changed for the better, and now I am living happily and healthily. The lesson is clear. Your fate is completely determined by what you hold in your heart."

We all want to do good work and lead good lives, and to do this we must always try to create something beautiful in our hearts. Thinking good thoughts will help to make our lives wonderful.

Elevating Your Mental Dimension

When Kyocera was first started, we had neither money nor equipment. In the midst of this I determined to base my management of the company on the human spirit. The human spirit is changeable, but once bound by trust, there is no stronger bond in the world. By feeling mutual trust while working alongside our colleagues, we can overcome any difficulty.

I worked hard to be a leader my employees could depend on. In order that my employees and I could become trusted friends, at every opportunity I got I said I wanted them to lift up their hearts a little. In this way, the entire company staff, including myself, worked hard to elevate our mental dimension, and I believe that our complete involvement in our work brought about the success of the Kyocera group.

At Kyocera, one resource for raising our mental dimension is the Kyocera Philosophy. This is a collection of thoughts that have occurred to me during my life and have been engraved into my heart at work. Today they fill a fairly hefty book. This philosophy contains the basis of our management policies, including "how to live as a human being" and "the spiritual approach to work." Here I'd like to introduce some important points relating to "what is the correct thing for a human being to do" and "making an effort."

First, with respect to the former, there are the following points:

"As human beings we must seek good."

When we are shown examples of wrongdoing and of the evil side of the world, we should think, "This should not be allowed. Human beings should not act this way." We should constantly ask ourselves, "What is the correct thing for a human being to do?" and should seek the answer.

Constantly maintaining a spirit of seeking out what is good is the same as continuously striving for our ideals. It should constitute the foundation of our lives.

"No matter what difficulties are involved, we must play fair in business and approach all transactions honestly."

It is crucial to uphold the fundamental principle, "Do what is the correct thing to do." Even if a new employee discovers an error, I want him to announce it properly and with dignity. People must be dedicated to fair play in business and to doing business with a good attitude. We must pursue the path of correctness in business.

"In our dealings, we must have sincerity, righteousness, courage, love, and humility in our hearts."

This is a necessary condition for determining what is the correct thing to do. We humans naturally tend to lean toward actions based on selfish instincts such as greed, arrogance, self-importance, jealousy, and remorse. Dealing with things in such a spirit will not produce the right decisions. We must overcome these "instincts" and hold in our hearts the sincerity, righteousness, courage, love, and humility that come from our souls.

These qualities are easy to talk about, but few people can make them the criteria by which they live. Those who can really do this will succeed in any field.

"Love must be the foundation of our actions."

Love should not be blind. If it is, it will cause harm rather than good, just as when a child is indulged through love, with disastrous results. Something that seems attractive at first may turn out to have terrible consequences. There are plenty of examples of things we thought were good but turned out to be bad. We need penetrating insight in order to learn to discriminate and distinguish what is really good We must act with love, but we should not regard this love as a simple matter.

"When modest, timid people acquire true courage, they achieve great things."

In corporate management or research and development or

any other field of business, people are constantly having to make decisions. Our current selves and the image of our company are the sum total of all these decisions. In some cases we must have the courage to make weighty decisions with far-reaching consequences. Such decisions require true courage, but not the sort of courage of a caveman. When a modest, timid person acquires experience and develops true courage, he becomes capable of making the correct decisions and achieving great things.

With regard to "making an effort," our corporate philosophy includes the following points:

"There is no limit to sincere effort. Such unlimited effort leads to inconceivably great things."

Great effort makes great things happen, but it must be a superhuman effort that exceeds anyone else's. If you say, "I've done so much, and that's enough," and work less hard than other people, you cannot succeed. If the other man works harder than you and you lose out to the competition, then you might as well not have worked at all. Effort knows no limits, no "this is enough." It is unlimited effort that accomplishes great things.

"It is not always possible to achieve great things from the outset. They come through continuous hard work and by taking one step at a time."

Once you have set your target, you will have to keep working hard every day to achieve it. People tend to think about big things all the time; so much so that when there's some trivial, daily matter to attend to, they think, "This little thing can't make any difference." If you brush off such small chores that way, you'll wind up full of remorse because of the huge gap that will appear between your goals and what you have actually accomplished.

at things, by definition, seem impossible to achieve at start. They are the products of plain, hard, consistent work, with the tasks tackled one at a time. It is crucial to keep on working hard, no matter how distant your goals may seem.

"Every time you take a step forward, the next step will become apparent. In this way great things are achieved."

Proceed step by step, like an inchworm. This is the way to take up the challenge of great things—not with some extravagant gesture, but with many small steps. In fact, each step may be so tiny you can't believe that it will amount to much, but these steps accumulate, and one day they will lead you to the success that is admired by everyone

"There are three types of material: that which burns with a fire lit by something outside, that which does not burn at all, and that which burns with its own fire. People who want to accomplish something great and important must have the passion to burn with their own fire."

Some objects are flammable; they take energy from elsewhere and use that energy to burn. Other things are non-flammable; you can't set them alight. And some things are self-starting: they burn all by themselves. People who create something exciting must have the power to burn by themselves.

To "burn" here means to burn with passion—that is, to love what you are doing. If it's something you like, you become caught up in it on your own initiative and work really hard at it. It also interests you because you like it, and you don't get tired of working on it. In order to burn on your initiative you must set goals for yourself. Once you have set your life goals or your company goals, you will burn with the desire to achieve them.

This is one part of the Kyocera Philosophy. Much of it, of

course, is rather obvious, but I seriously try to live by these guidelines, and I constantly tell my employees that I want them to be just as serious about them. So far my employees have understood me and have been consistently working hard to follow me.

In this way, Kyocera, which was founded by eight colleagues with similar values, grew into three business groups: the Kyocera group, the DDI communications group, and the Taito group in the entertainment industry. Our enterprises now employ more than 33,000 people. Even during the current recession, these groups have recorded sales totaling around US$14 billion per year, and profit of more than US$2.2 billion.

These phenomenal achievements are the result of every one of our employees striving from the start to elevate one another's mental outlook and to work with a clean and pure heart. Even I am surprised by how wonderful my life now is. I think a lot of employees feel the same way.

A Formula for Life
As a manager aware of spiritual dimensions, I have come to think that one's life depends on three factors, which can be expressed in a formula:

$$\text{Achievement} = \text{Ability} \times \text{Effort} \times \text{Way of Thinking}.$$

One of these, "ability," refers to one's inborn talents, including one's physical health. Ability is a God-given gift that cannot be changed. The next factor, "effort," means dedication and involves the strong will to achieve something, no matter at what cost. Effort is affected by what you hold in your heart.

Ability and effort may vary on a scale from 0 to 100, but what counts is the product of the two. Therefore, even if you have the same ability as a self-assured person who doesn't work hard, if you work harder and with a greater passion, you will achieve far better results.

Finally, one's "way of thinking" is important as well. It refers to the spiritual dimension of your life work, and it varies on a scale from −100 to +100. Negative thoughts such as anger, jealousy, and hate result in a negative figure, whereas positive thoughts lead to a positive score.

There are two crucial aspects that are worthy of noting in this Formula for Life. First, it involves multiplication; and second, the "way of thinking" can be either a plus or a minus figure. As ability and effort increase, the results will be multiplied. However, if you cannot view things in a positive light and your mindset is even slightly negative, your total achievement, too, will become negative. Conversely, a positive mindset will lead to positive achievements. To lead a good life, it is essential to have a positive and optimistic mindset.

It is interesting that much the same philosophy was espoused by Yukichi Fukuzawa (1835–1901), one of the founding fathers of modern Japan—the man whose face now adorns the ¥10,000 bill. During the Meiji era, when Japan threw out its feudal system in order to become a modern nation, Fukuzawa visited Europe and America to observe the industries and the economies there. After he returned to Japan, he predicted that such industries would also come to Japan, and he wrote about the type of man who should be a leader of industry: "Take the deep thoughts of the philosopher and the samurai's deep integrity. Add to these the talents of a government official and the body of a farmer. Only then will you have a leader of industry."

When Fukuzawa refers to "the deep thoughts of a philosopher," he means that a leader must have the kind of deep and probing mind a philosopher has. "The deep integrity of a samurai" means that a leader's spirit must be as dignified and selfless as that of the warriors of "Chushingura," the famous tale of forty-seven samurai who held true to their oath of service even after their master's death. "The talents of a government official" means a shrewdness that is essential for business.

With the establishment of the new Meiji government, the number of administrators increased rapidly, and many of them were probably sharp, shrewd men. Finally, "the body of a farmer" means that a healthy, strong body and the ability to endure are also essential. In summary, Fukuzawa meant that the three elements necessary to a captain of industry are a sound mind, a sound body, and a sharp business sense.

Applying this to my Formula for Life, depth of thought and integrity of spirit correspond to the "way of thinking." The talents of a government official correspond to "ability." And the healthy body of a farmer corresponds to "effort." It follows that no business can succeed without these qualities. Life works the same way.

Chapter

11

Creating a Spiritual Dimension

In daily life we often talk of the "spiritual" aspect of life, although few people can really explain what this "spirit" refers to. Yet without understanding it, it is difficult to think realistically about such questions as "What is a human being?" or "How should we live?" It seems relevant at this point to discuss the concept of this spiritual dimension to life.

I believe that within the human spirit exists something called a "soul." The soul is continually reborn and carries with it the entire history of its past lives. The previous experiences of the soul are called "karma" in Buddhist philosophy. I believe that in our spirits exists the soul that carries this "karma" with it.

The human spirit is not composed entirely of this soul. Outside of the soul there is the rational element (the frontal lobe of the brain), which we use to think. In the next layer come the emotions, then the sensations (the five senses). And the outermost layer, wrapped around the others, is what could be called instinct. I believe that the human spirit is composed of all these layers: beginning from the inside and moving outward, the soul, the rational element, emotions, sensations, and instinct.

154

If one thinks of the human spirit as being con
this way, then its most important constituent is the
at the very center. So what is the soul? I believe th
self—that is, the innermost, true self that accom
physical selves. Practitioners of Zen engage in th.. ....
zazen—that is, silent meditation—in order to see the true substance of the self in its entirety. If you do zazen and keep up
this probing, it is said that you will arrive at the Zen conclusion: all existence is "air." This is what is meant by "Matter is
void. All is vanity." It is said that also by doing yoga and meditating on what the self really is, you can touch the true self.

In Buddhist thinking, achieving contact with the true self is
called nirvana, or the state of total immersion, and it is said to
be a state of indescribable bliss. This nirvana may be a fleeting
experience, or one that lasts thirty minutes to an hour. The
famous Japanese Zen priest Hakuin (1685–1768) is said to have
experienced "eighteen big nirvanas and innumerable small
nirvanas."

In this way, people who come into contact with their souls
and achieve nirvana through ascetic practices, zazen, or meditation are overflowing with love. They are imbued with empathy; that is, they are happier when other people succeed than
when they themselves succeed. This is because they have been
able to come into contact with the soul, which overflows with
kindness.

Some people don't believe in the soul, but if we humans
don't have souls, then our spirits are composed only of
instinct, the emotions, the sensations that come from our five
senses, and the rational thinking that takes place in the cere-
brum. A truly rewarding life, however, requires something
more than just emotions, sensations, and rational thinking.

To lead a truly fulfilling and wonderful life, a spiritual
dimension is necessary. For example, when we see a troubled
person we think, "I'd like to help somehow." The fact that our
spirit is filled with this generosity makes us feel refreshed and

happy. To achieve the goals we set for ourselves, we need to have an intense fighting spirit. We need to be able to avoid frustration no matter what disaster besets us, no matter how sick we get. This simply cannot come from instinct, emotions, sensations, or rational thought. It is something that springs from the soul. Without that "something" emanating from the soul, it is impossible to lead a fulfilling life.

Actually, we come face to face with our souls in childhood. Everyone has had the experience of doing something naughty when a child and thinking, "I wonder if I'll get caught?" "I wonder if Mom will scold me?" "I shouldn't have done it." Children are pure, and without thinking their souls—their consciences—are revealed on their faces. When we grow up we lose the pangs of conscience and this pure spirit. When humans become dishonest, their souls are suppressed.

What we normally feel are our selfish tendencies, the emotions and sensations of our daily lives, and the rational element that attempts to control all of them. Unfortunately, we are rarely aware of the soul that is at the core of our spirit. However, unless you believe in this soul and understand its importance, it is impossible for you to think about what it means to be human being or what it is important to hold in our hearts.

The Changeable and the Unchangeable Spirit

If you observe the state of your spirit, you will find that it contains both changeable and unchangeable elements. The changeable elements are probably those closest to human nature, and the unchangeable ones are probably closest to the soul. I'd like to give a couple of examples to explain this. On the human level, eating a sumptuous banquet should make us feel satisfied and happy, but if you eat the same kind of meal the next day, and the day after that, you will gradually start to dislike it. Even though you might have been delighted to have a single potato to eat at some time in the past, as you slowly get used to luxury you can't even become excited about a banquet. This is one aspect of human nature.

At this level, our desires take over and grow unchecked. If all people try to attain happiness by satisfying their desires, which are boundless, the energy and resources of the entire planet will be insufficient. Happiness experienced at this level is not constant but momentary—a bubble that quickly bursts. Then this happiness gradually turns to boredom, and desire grows correspondingly.

The happiness experienced at the level of sensation is similar. Take listening to a symphony. The first time you hear a piece of music you may be overcome with emotion, but as you listen to it many times you may start to think, "This performance isn't so brilliant." It's the same with paintings: after you've seen many good ones, you may look at a painting that used to strike you as wonderful and think, "This work really isn't that great." As your perceptions become sharper, your standards also start to change. Things that used to impress you increasingly fail to make you feel that way. The same is true at the emotional level.

A similar process occurs in the realm of rational thought. Take the example of a theory in physics. At one time, Newton's laws were thought to be correct, but now scientists contend that they are insufficient to explain all phenomena. In other words, science, too, is changing day by day. Nothing can be permanently correct, without change, for all time. Thus, even the rational element of the human spirit is mutable. So where is stability? What is there that will not change? Ultimately, this is only found at the level of the soul.

What kind of things are felt at the level of the soul? Usually they lie beyond rational comprehension, but occasionally they appear in a form we can understand.

For example, think about what really makes a person attractive. We may look at someone on the rational or instinctive level and think, "He's not an attractive person," or "He has no talent." And yet we may still be attracted to such a person on the spiritual level. On the other hand, we would feel no attraction whatsoever to a highly talented, good-looking person who is cold toward others and thinks only of himself.

True attractiveness comes not from good looks or talents but from human kindness. When we meet a person overflowing with kindness, we feel happy and our hearts are comforted. Why should this be so?

As I explained before, it is because our souls are filled with kindness, and our souls are drawn to people of the same sort. No matter how many times we meet that person, we still feel warmth and happiness. Our souls are responsible for this, and this part of our spirit will never change.

The human spirit consists of transient and permanent elements. We should not be obsessed with the transient outer layers of our spirit. Rather we should regard the unchanging element at the core as the most important. We should avoid being engrossed in the physical side of things and instead strive to look for true substance with the aid of our souls.

Our Souls Indicate Where Happiness Lies

The soul I have been talking about overflows with love, sincerity, and harmony, which can be expressed with the words "truth," "happiness," and "beauty." Jesus Christ spoke of "love," and the Buddha of "compassion." These qualities are represented by the "soul" I speak of. We would do well to believe simply and implicitly in these qualities. If we live in accordance with them, we will find true happiness.

As many religions teach, it is by striving for sincerity, modesty, innocence, and kindness that we may approach the true essence of the soul and lead good lives. On the other hand, if we approach everything with frustration, jealousy, hatred, and anger, nothing in our lives will go smoothly. We should be faithful to our souls, and in doing so, we may lead spiritually rewarding lives.

This soul is not something that is only possessed by human beings. All living creatures have a soul, and our souls have existed since the beginning of the world. The most convincing theory of the birth of the cosmos is the big bang theory, which says that in the beginning there was a clump of elementary particles, which exploded and scattered to form the entire universe. According to this theory, after the big explosion, elementary particles combined to form neutrons and protons, which were bound by mesons to form atomic nuclei. From electrons, with a nucleus at the center, the first atom was formed. Then, as these atoms combined, heavier atoms came into being, and these combined to create molecules and polymers, from which proteins and other matter developed. These received some kind of energy and became life forms, evolving into tiny organisms. These organisms further evolved into the plant and animal kingdoms, and finally human beings came into existence.

The point of all this is that elementary particles do not exist as elementary particles forever. They gradually become more and more complex. All things are continually advancing, developing, and evolving, without an instant's pause. At this point I feel the existence of a kindness filled with a positive goodwill. In other words, in our universe there is something called the "law of love." With the help of love, all things flow in the direction of evolution and maturity. The universe is filled with love.

Naturally, all human beings and the world they live in are part of the universal "law of love." Our souls are filled with kindness, so they are founded on love, in accordance with the law of the universe. And when applied to the human world, the law of love of the universe becomes "the law that all people move in the direction of happiness."

If we live in accordance with the universal law of love, if we move in the direction our souls indicate, if we work hard with innocence, modesty, and generosity, nothing will keep us from leading wonderful, fulfilling lives. If something goes wrong, we can assume, modestly and regretfully, that there was an element in our spirit that violated the law of love.

If we overcome the human tendency to get caught up in the insignificant physical world, if we live our lives modestly, at some point we will come to understand our true selves in the vast universe. The essential requirements of a good life are to live in accordance with the universal law of love and to fill our hearts with kindness.

Caring for Others

I believe the human spirit can be roughly divided into two parts: one that cares for others, and the other that cares for oneself. The part that cares for oneself is satisfied so long as one is all right, but the part that cares for others seeks to help others even at the sacrifice of oneself.

Human beings must eat every day in order to survive. After ten days without food, most people will die. This physical appetite is part of the spirit that cares for oneself. The desire to procreate and leave behind descendants, the appetite for fame, the wish to be well thought of, and the feelings of anger, hatred, and jealousy are all part of the spirit that cares for oneself. The first human beings only had this spirit and made decisions based solely on what was convenient for themselves and whether they profited or suffered.

When expressed in this way, you may think this "selfish" spirit is at best a necessary evil, but this is not completely true. Indeed, the spirit of caring for oneself is necessary to sustain life, and this is one of the reasons why we are endowed with it. Interestingly though, caring for oneself is not enough. If we only satisfy this selfish spirit and think that "as long as I'm all right, all is well," we will never find happiness or fulfillment in life.

Take the example of running a business. Suppose a manager's motives in running his business are his selfish desires only—to increase the company's profits and make his own lifestyle more luxurious. Things might go well at first, but this will not last. At some point the company will inevitably collapse. The man who thinks that all is well as long as he is all right will eventually take some antisocial step and antagonize the public. There will be a backlash from society as a whole, severe friction will develop, and the manager will be in great trouble.

Indeed, more than a few people who were once considered great managers have wound up beset by disaster. They began to think only of their own company's welfare; they began to want power for its own sake in a period when they were becoming more famous and therefore should have been widening their managerial horizons. In recent years, Japan has seen frequent disgraceful affairs such as financial scandals and cases of bribery in the construction industry. Many managers have been kicked out of companies to which they have devoted half their lives. I feel this is because, at some point, they succumbed to the comfortable belief that everything was all right as long as they and their company were doing well.

This does not only apply to business but is valid in every area of life. Many people suffer repeated failures because they let their selfish interests get out of hand. The spirit of caring for oneself is necessary, but with that spirit alone one cannot lead a good life. We must make the happiness of others our own happiness, the misfortune of others our own misfortune; in other words, we need the spirit of caring for others. The spirit of caring for oneself and the spirit of caring for others are complementary elements in the human spirit. Our lives are greatly influenced by which of the two we decide to emphasize in our conduct.

The Difference between Heaven and Hell

I heard the following story from the chief priest of the temple of Enfuku-ji in Kyoto. Since it is a nice illustration of the importance of the spirit of caring for others, let me repeat it here.

An itinerant monk once asked a priest, "They say the other world consists of heaven and hell, but is that really so? And if hell exists, what kind of place is it?"

The priest replied, "Of course the other world consists of heaven and hell, but they are not as different as you think. From the outside, heaven and hell look precisely the same. The difference lies in the spirit of the people who are in them. People who only care about themselves are in hell. People who care about others are in paradise."

The monk then asked, "How are heaven and hell distinguished by the spirit of their inhabitants?"

To this the priest replied with the following parable. In the middle of a room there are two big pots, one filled with noodles and the other filled with hot broth for the noodles. People can help themselves to all they want—but they must abide by certain rules. They have to eat the noodles with yard-long chopsticks, and they can only use the tips of the chopsticks to pick up the noodles. The size of the pots and the number of people around them are the same in each room. In other words, this scenario is the same whether in hell or in paradise. The only difference lies in the spirit of the people.

"Now," continued the priest, "imagine what happens when you are hungry and someone brings delicious noodles into the room and says to you, 'Go ahead and eat!' You are quick to seize the noodles with your meter-long chopsticks and you dip them in the broth in the other pot. However, you can't bring the noodles to your mouth because the chopsticks are longer than your arm. And everyone gathered around the pots is thinking, 'If this guy eats it all, there won't be any left for us.' So they try to pull the noodles off your chopsticks with theirs. It is a terrible scene. The noodles you wanted so much to eat fall all around the pot, and nobody gets even a bite. Despite plenty of noodles and broth being available, everybody is trapped in a hell of hunger.

"In heaven, on the other hand, the people say, 'The noodles are ready. Let's all eat together.' And one person uses his chopsticks to pick up some noodles from the pot. He dips these in the broth and says, "Please, you eat first." And he holds out the chopsticks and lets someone on the other side of the room eat. That person says, "That was delicious! Now it's your turn," and the person who just ate offers the other person some noodles. Not one strand of noodles falls to the floor, and everybody eats his fill. All help one another—and all are able to eat.

"At first glance, the room looks just like the room in hell," said the priest, "but it is heaven."

This parable makes clear the difference between caring only for oneself and caring for others. The way you hold these concepts in your heart is the difference between heaven and hell.

Concern for Others Expands Your Horizons

By caring for others in this way, our horizons widen and we no longer encounter serious setbacks. For example, if a manager works hard to ensure that all his employees have stable jobs and lives, even as the company expands and his employees multiply, then his spirit of concern for other people will increase accordingly. And if he goes on to make an additional contribution, however small, to his local community, his spirit of concern for others will extend further, to include the town where he lives. Then, if he tries to help, even just a little, his nation and the international community, his spirit will become even larger. The kind spirit of a manager is thus not confined to his own employees but spreads out to the area, to the nation, and eventually to the international community.

Here I should mention that there is an inverse relationship

between caring for others and caring for oneself. Take, for example, a small company. If the manager of it decides to protect the company and make the employees his top priority, he has a spirit of concern for others. But if he cares only about the company, then from the viewpoint of society this is nothing more than self-interest, since only the company will benefit. He may think that as long as the company doing all right, all is well—but in so thinking he is working against society.

To take the example further, if a resident of a certain area starts to think not just about his family but also about the local community, then he has a spirit of concern for others. But if it stops there, or if it is only the local society he cares about, then from the viewpoint of the nation it is nothing but local selfishness. If his caring spirit expands to include his nation, this, too, is nothing more than self-interest for his country. Pursuing only national welfare is damaging to the rest of the world. In other words, a concern for local or national welfare is not sufficient; a wider spirit of global welfare is required.

This example demonstrates an important truth, i.e., the farther you extend your concern for others, the farther your own horizons will expand. As your concern for others spreads outward, from caring about yourself to holding your family important, to making your company better, to improving your local community, to working for your nation, and finally to contributing to the global community, your interest in these areas increases accordingly and your horizons widen.

As your horizons grow in this way, you will begin to see "beyond the present" and you will start to make correct decisions. Even before any problem arises, you will be able to take appropriate preventive action. On the other hand, if you allow yourself to get caught up in self-interest, you will only think about yourself, and your horizons will become extremely narrow. You will start making decisions based on the short term, and ultimately you will fail.

It is good to increase our spirit of concern for others, even if only slightly. By so doing we are not only able to lead lives of happiness and spiritual richness, but our horizons also widen and enable us to see into the future.

Make Concern for Others the Basis of Your Actions

Every day a person makes many decisions, ranging from those concerning minor details to those about matters of great importance. None of these decisions is 100 percent correct, and none is 100 percent wrong. And each day sees the accumulation of decisions at levels between minor and major. The accumulated results of all the decisions we have made up until the present are what make up our current life. In other words, the sum total of our daily actions and decisions defines our life.

How do these decisions come about? What do we use as the basis for our decisions? Some things we decide immediately and impulsively; other things we discuss with friends before deciding. There are many approaches to decision-making, but if you think about it, ultimately it is our spirit that really makes the decisions. The basis for decision-making lies in the human spirit.

Within the human spirit, as I explained earlier, there are many levels. First of all, in some cases our decisions are made subconsciously, at the instinctive level. As human nature is fundamentally self-centered, its criterion for decisions is based only on whether one stands to gain or lose.

Next, there are instances when we make decisions based on emotions or sensations, through the five senses. In this case, the criteria for our decisions change easily and often lack consistency. They change according to our experiences and habits, and our decisions are influenced by our physical state and the environment around us.

Other decisions are made on the rational level. The rational element of the human spirit analyzes the real world and draws logical conclusions. We may use this element to analyze situations, but this often does not result in any action. Our rational part accepts current situations as they are, so it is not much help in deciding when things need to be changed and how to make such changes.

Finally, some decisions are made by the innermost part of the spirit, which is embedded deeper than the rational element. This innermost core is the soul—that is, the spirit of concern for others. It is the spirit that overcomes selfish concerns and is willing to make sacrifices for the sake of others. Decisions made by the soul are based on the notion of "whatever is best for others." This is equivalent to the universal law of love I introduced earlier, so it does not cause friction with anything. It is joyously accepted by everybody. It is a force that can motivate people.

Considering that our life is the total accumulation of our daily decisions, we should try our best to base our decisions on the spirit of concern for others, in other words, according to the law of love. If we succeed in doing this, then everybody around us will accept our decisions wholeheartedly and will cooperate with us. Then everything will go smoothly and well. By accumulating many such decisions each day, we will enrich our life, making it truly wonderful.

Japan arose from the ruins of the war to become one of the strongest economic powers in the world. Throughout this period, the Japanese people worked hard. Yet other people in the world are not happy with our success, and it has not made them trust or respect the Japanese more. At the same time, the ordinary Japanese is not able to regard this success with pride. Why is this?

I feel that although Japan has achieved economic success, the Japanese have been trapped by largely selfish values because a lot of people do not know when enough is enough. They insist on satisfying their desires, which grow endlessly.

Consider the many politicians, bureaucrats, and business managers who were tainted by the infamous "Recruit scandal"—when a greedy corporation paid huge bribes to political insiders—and again through the financial industry scandals, the bribery cases in the construction industry, and so on. Consider all the salaried men who tried to get rich quick during the "bubble" era and wound up going bankrupt or nearly so. There is no shortage of examples of people who ruined themselves out of their selfish greed.

When politicians, bureaucrats, financiers, and even salaried workers get caught up in caring only for themselves, they lose sight of how a human being should behave and work only to satisfy their greed. Japan's current state of national confusion, I believe, stems from the fact that people have only cared for themselves. What we now need is a new way of life, one based on a spirit of concern for others.

Extending the Spirit of Concern for Others
As I have emphasized throughout this book, the spirit of concern for others is of the utmost importance, but it is not easy to cultivate. This is because the soul lies in the deepest, innermost region of the spirit and is hard to make contact with.

To call forth your soul takes deep meditation. As I mentioned before, even the Zen priest Hakuin, who spent his entire life meditating and following the way of the Buddha, came into contact with his soul—that is, achieved nirvana— only eighteen times. So for an average person, occupied with the trivialities of daily life, it is particularly difficult to meditate and contact the soul. Consequently, it is equally difficult to cultivate our spirit of concern for others. Even if we try to maintain a pure spirit and want to think and act for the benefit of others, this generous attitude is not easy to achieve.

In my view, to the extent we can control our concern for ourselves, a corresponding quantity of concern for others will emerge. It is as if the human spirit were a vase filled with selfish impulses. The more we reduce our selfishness, the more space there will be inside the vase to be filled with the spirit of generosity. That's how the human spirit works.

It is not necessary to "kill" ourselves in our attempts to be concerned about others. All we have to do is control our self-ishness. According to Buddhist thought, controlling that self-ish spirit is called "Being content with what you have." If we let our desires run unchecked, they will grow without limit. By always keeping in mind that enough is enough, we can learn to control them. And once we do this, a spirit of concern for others will naturally emerge.

Takamori Saigo, the famous nineteenth-century samurai who became a leader of the Meiji era reforms (and who is, inci-dentally, one of the local heroes of my hometown of Kago-shima), left behind the following advice about controlling one's selfishness.

Loving yourself is the worst thing of all. People who can't meditate, people who can't do anything successfully, peo-ple who can't correct their mistakes, and people who are arrogant and boast of their success are like this only because they love themselves, which means ultimately that they do not love themselves.

Living a Life of Self-Awareness

One of our goals is, I believe, to seek to elevate our spiritual or mental dimension. There are two ways of doing this. One opportunity arises when we face a very serious difficulty—one that may affect our life or threaten our reputation—for exam-ple, when we contract a serious illness and come close to death, or when we are taken to court for some wrongdoing or undergo a similar experience that causes people to look down upon us. By having such traumatic experiences and suffering through them, people change. They can be transformed and can achieve nirvana. However, this is a passive method since we cannot induce the necessary circumstances by ourselves.

The other method is to be aware, always, of our own human shortcomings. By living a life of introspection and contemplation, our stature as human beings will be raised. Through repeated examination of ourselves and our actions, our subconscious—a crucial element of our composition—will be altered.

In this method, we are the active instigator, and anybody can do it. To succeed in it, it is crucial to have a strong determination and desire to make our character more noble. For normal people like us to elevate our humanity, a strong will is essential, and we must continually contemplate and question our way of life.

Incidentally, no matter how much we have succeeded in elevating our character, we must continue with our modest contemplation in order to be able to maintain it at that level. For example, suppose we read a book whose content impresses us a great deal. This will raise the level of our spirit. However, it is momentary, and if we don't continue receiving similar sorts of stimulation, we will not be able to maintain that level. Even for a person with an extremely kind heart for whom everything has gone well—if such a person neglects contemplation, his way of thinking will decline and he will revert to being a self-centered person.

Sometimes, in the religious world, a person engages in intense meditation in his youth and becomes an excellent priest. Then in later life he stops meditating and returns to being simply a normal man. No matter how high we elevate our spirit, if we do not maintain continuous contemplation and study, we will, like the priest, revert to our original state: this is the nature of humanity. It is similar to an athlete who has trained hard every day to build an outstanding body; if he neglects his training, even slightly, then his well-conditioned body will deteriorate. To elevate your humanity requires much study and learning, and serious contemplation.

Some believe it is possible to elevate oneself through education, but I feel education alone is insufficient. Education teaches us how to think rationally, but when we act, we tend to skip the rational and act on instinct. In other words, our self-interest surfaces. We take inexcusable actions in direct opposition to what we were taught. What we learn through education can be likened to a foundation, but to build on it we need to be continually aware of our shortcomings.

Awareness of our humanity means a life of constant and humble contemplation, and of continually examining our feelings and asking whether the decisions we make are correct. We must look inside ourselves and say, "Don't think only of yourself like that," or "Don't be such a coward." By repeatedly reviewing our own conduct in this way, we can catch ourselves before we make mistakes, and eventually learn not to make mistakes.

In the hustle and bustle of daily life, we are quick to lose sight of ourselves. To prevent this, we must make a conscious habit of contemplating our actions. By living a life of genuine self-awareness, we may correct the flaws in our characters and elevate our stature as human beings.

The Kyoto Prizes

The Kyoto Prizes have been awarded each year since 1985, so this is their twelfth year. The recipients of the prizes this year were as follows. The Advanced Technology Prize was awarded to Donald E. Knuth, the American computer scientist who has made numerous contributions to the development of the information sciences. The Basic Sciences Prize was presented to Mario R. Capecchi of the University of Utah, who developed the "gene targeting" technique now widely used around the world. The prize for Creative Arts and Moral Sciences went to Willard Van Orman Quine, professor emeritus at Harvard University, who has created a new paradigm of philosophy for the second half of the twentieth century. The three prizewinners each received a commemorative medal and the sum of ¥50,000,000 (about US$500,000).

I first conceived the idea of the Kyoto Prizes in 1984, when

Kyocera celebrated the twenty-fifth anniversary of its foundation. Having started with nothing, Kyocera had developed into a top-rank company through the hard work of its employees and the support of people in general. I was eager to give something back, and I wanted to bring to life the concept that "Making something for the benefit of the world is the greatest act a human being can perform."

I was aware that there were many researchers who had never gained recognition for their hard work and achievements, since there were few international prizes awarded. Recognizing the efforts of such people—who have devoted themselves to making a contribution to the world—is a worthy cause, and it was something I had long wished to do, so I donated some US$200 million to create the Inamori Foundation and launch the Kyoto Prizes. At the time I was fifty-two years old. Some people thought highly of it, but others criticized me for it, calling me "saucy" for creating this award. Some people even said that it was just a publicity stunt.

I have seen many people in the financial world who, when young, were filled with idealism but fell prey to self-interest as they grew older and became greedy old men. Frankly, that US$200 million I gave was a large sum that I had worked hard to earn. As a normal human being, I was sorry to part with it, but at the time I thought it would be my only chance at this sort of undertaking.

I decided that recipients of the Kyoto Prizes had to be people who had humbly devoted themselves to hard work—as we at Kyocera had done. I wanted to honor those who had struggled to find the right path in the wilderness, and thus made great contributions in the fields of culture, science, and philosophy. I wanted to honor people whose hard work stemmed from a desire to bring happiness to mankind.

The Kyoto Prizes are fairly close to what I had hoped for when I planned them. They have been awarded to remarkable men and women who have worked for the common good—

and received little recognition worldwide. When I see the attention and praise these phenomenal achievers receive after being awarded the Kyoto Prizes, I feel I have accomplished a wonderful thing.

However, I want to avoid the suggestion that I am the sole person responsible for the Kyoto Prizes. They were made possible through the advice of many of Japan's leading experts in various fields, through the assistance of both the national government and the Kyoto prefectural and city governments, and through the many citizens who warmly welcomed the awards. Once again I would like to express my gratitude to all of them.

I had no intention of making this book a record of my own achievements. I am just an ordinary person who was lucky enough to find success and make an unbelievable amount of money. Whenever I tell myself, "I earned all this money," my conscience whispers back, "No, you didn't. You have the world to thank." So I fervently try to control my selfishness and do something, however small, for the world and humanity. In so doing I have made a lot of people happy, and my life since has become even more rewarding.

This is exactly the message that I want to get across in this book. I feel that I have learned all over again that the true way to a rewarding life is to foster that inner spirit of concern for others—no matter how much hard work or money it takes. And this is a truth that applies equally to all human beings.

THE REFORM OF JAPAN

The Reform of Japan*

D uring the three years from 1991 to 1993, I was a member of the third Provisional Council for the Promotion of Administrative Reform, chaired by Eiji Suzuki, the late president of the Nikkeiren (Japan Federation of Employers' Associations). For the first half of this period, I was chairman of the committee on "Japan and the World," where we discussed such topics as what basic principles should guide Japan's foreign policy and how Japan should relax various regulations. During the second half of this period, I chaired the "Re-examination of the Role of Government" committee, which made recommendations to the government on such subjects as the restructuring of special public corporations.

I believe I have identified three major areas that deserve consideration for reform. First, enact legislative reform to create a smaller government with lower taxes. Second, take drastic steps to remove regulatory constraints and lower the cost of

---

* Adapted from a speech given to the Keizai Doyukai (Japan Committee for Economic Development) at the Rihga Royal Hotel Hiroshima on March 14, 1996.

177

living. Third, revitalize local communities through the decentralization of power.

During the three years that I was a member of the council, more generally known as the Administrative Reform Council, or the ARC, I had opportunities to meet a large number of government officials and to gain a better understanding of how the country operates. Quite frankly, I had a lot to learn about the mechanisms of Japan's politics, administration, and bureaucratic structure. I was particularly alarmed when I realized how bureaucratically Japan is managed. The system might even be called a "bureaucratic dictatorship." Japan supports policies that depend on bureaucrats, whose central aim is maintaining the status quo and promoting economic development without considering the wishes of the public.

Of our committee's three proposals, I shall first focus on the last one, that of delegating more power to regional governments. Although the proposal has the potential to revitalize local communities, it obviously weakens the power of the central government. For this reason, it soon became painfully obvious to me that no bureaucrat would be interested in implementing such a reform. What I learned through my experiences on the ARC was that we cannot expect to use the power of the bureaucrats themselves to weaken the authority of the bureaucracy.

You may ask how and why did such a bureaucratic leadership, or "bureaucratic dictatorship," come into being. To understand this, we must look back through the history of Japan since World War II. As we all know, the defeat of Japan resulted in the Occupation of Japan by the Allied forces. Headed by General Douglas MacArthur, the Occupation attempted to modernize Japan by abolishing its armed forces and disbanding its huge industrial conglomerates. However, to avoid adding to the postwar confusion, it retained the administrative system, which was run by Japan's bureaucrats. Thus, the powerful bureaucratic structure of prewar Japan was left intact.

From the end of the war in 1945 through the first half of the 1950s, Japan was economically very weak. Socialists and communists were agitating among the populace, creating a major ideological conflict and causing much chaos and confusion on the political scene. The 1960s saw the rise of an opposition movement against the renewal of the U.S.–Japan Security Treaty. Public opinion was divided, and Japanese society was in turmoil.

Had Japan's political system been decided by the whim of the populace in this unstable social situation, Japan would have become a communist country by the end of the 1950s or early 1960s. That would have been a very unfortunate turn of events for the general public. It is understandable that our government officials began to think of themselves as the pure-minded and intellectually astute guardians of the nation's development.

In this way, the bureaucrats began to formulate the policies that they considered to be in the best interests of national economic development, and they abandoned worrying about adhering to democratic principles or reflecting popular opinion. This bureaucratic management was an effective mechanism for social and economic development, and it brought wonderful results in the five decades after the war. Had Japan not had such a powerful bureaucratic structure, it is doubtful that it would have become as prosperous as it is today. Thus, I have to admit that the existence of this bureaucratic leadership in the political and administrative system was fortunate for the people during those unsettled times.

On the other hand, we must also admit that true democracy has not taken firm root in Japan. Even today, the system that developed under the extraordinary postwar social conditions continues to allow bureaucrats to decide all policies—despite the fact that our society has matured and this outdated system is widely recognized to be the cause of many of Japan's present problems.

The Realities of Japan's Political System

Democracy is based on the doctrine that sovereignty rests with the people. A democratic government should be of the people, by the people, and for the people. However, in Japan the bureaucrats are conducting politics in a way that makes us feel government exists separately from the people.

This becomes obvious, for example, when we examine the function and workings of the Diet and the cabinet, the most important organs in Japan's parliamentary democracy. The latest laws and budgets, which are largely concerned with the standard of living, should have been decided through serious discussion within the Diet, the country's highest political body. In reality, however, they are all decided by the bureaucrats and merely endorsed by the Diet after the fact. We might even go so far as to say that there are practically no laws that are authored and legislated by our national representatives.

Since Japan's elected representatives participate in the cabinet—the highest administrative power—we might be excused for believing that this organ would respect the will of the people. Unfortunately, that is not the case. Since the end of the war, a mechanism has existed whereby all proposals are first screened in a regular meeting of the vice-ministers of the ministries. Only proposals that receive the unanimous approval of the members can be presented at a cabinet meeting. In other words, only proposals considered harmless to the bureaucrats are presented. No cabinet member, it seems, wants to oppose this system out of fear of antagonizing the bureaucracy.

I have not personally observed a cabinet meeting, but from what I have heard unofficially, it is a mere formality. The chief cabinet secretary presents the proposals that have already been unanimously approved at the vice-ministers' meeting, and everybody listens and then gives his blessing. This is quite different from a true democratic government, where representatives elected by the people formulate and conduct policies on behalf of the people.

The bureaucrats, unfortunately, do not seem to trust the people. Although other nations consider that Japan has both a high education level and a society that is quite mature, the bureaucrats seem worried that, if they leave things to the private sector and natural market forces, the country's social order will collapse. They seem to believe they are the self-appointed guardians of Japan's existing social order.

In my own analysis of this bureaucratic dictatorship, the first salient feature is that once a policy has been decided by the bureaucrats, it must be protected unchanged, even if it later becomes clear that it was a mistake. It seems the bureaucrats believe that if they admit their mistakes and change their policies, the authority and prestige of the nation will be harmed.

A good example of this is seen in the recent dispute over the formula for settling the bankruptcies of the *"jusen"* housing loan companies. Once the settlement formula was decided, no effort was made to change it, even though virtually the entire population is opposed to it. Another case is seen in the spread of HIV infection among hemophiliacs. When we examine why and how the infection became widespread and scrutinize the actions of the Ministry of Health and Welfare, we find once again that it seems almost impossible to change any decision once it has been made, no matter how wrong it may have been.

The second salient feature of this bureaucratic dictatorship is that it is the bureaucrats who make the laws and not the elected representatives of the people. The bureaucrats consider themselves superior to the general public and think that it is up to them to legislate or change laws according to what they believe serves the best economic interests of the nation. In fact, they don't even have to legislate; they merely have to issue "administrative guidance" or "rulings" to have their decisions implemented. They may even defy existing laws and regulations on the pretext of safeguarding social order and stability.

The third salient feature is that the bureaucrats always adopt, as the central theme of their policies, the "protection and nurturing" of producers and suppliers of goods and services. Even when this is contrary to the interests of consumers, they will insist on policies that give priority to protecting suppliers and producers.

Issues in the Financial and Industrial Sectors

Japan sacrificed a huge number of its human resources in World War II. Furthermore, the end of the war brought about the purging of militarist or nationalist leaders from official positions. Due to these events, the leadership of the financial world was suddenly transferred to the shoulders of the younger generation.

In the harsh postwar economic climate, the young managers ran their companies by dint of hard work and constant study. In those unsettled times, many managers realized the need to polish their skills, so they organized study groups and established the philosophy and principles they considered necessary for leaders. One such group is the Keizai Doyukai association of corporate executives.

Thus, the managers of that period were not merely concerned with seeking their own profit. Rather, they were people who had a philosophy of leadership and were seriously concerned about the welfare of the entire population. And while they recognized the importance of cooperating with bureaucrats to develop the nation's economy, many did not hesitate to fight against policies they considered problematic. To give two examples, I can name Yotaro Nishiyama of Kawasaki Steel Corporation, who overrode opposition from the Bank of Japan to build high-temperature kilns, and Soichiro Honda of Honda Motor Co., Ltd., who fought the Ministry of International Trade and Industry (MITI) and won the right to start the production of Honda passenger cars.

There were many other admirable managers, such as Konosuke Matsushita of Matsushita Electric Industrial Co., Ltd., Takeshi Sakurada of Nisshinbo Industries, Inc., Kazutaka Kikawada of the Tokyo Electric Power Co., Inc., Sazo Idemitsu of Idemitsu Kosan Co., Ltd., and Toshio Doko of Ishikawa-jima-Harima Heavy Industries Co., Ltd. These people did not base their operations merely on profit. They managed their companies according to a management philosophy based on basic truths and ethical principles.

Now that these business leaders are no longer with us, the center stage is taken by younger people like me, who started business after Japan became a wealthy nation. To be candid, I, and perhaps many others, tend to kowtow to bureaucrats for our own benefit, and our operations are based on giving the highest priority to our own companies or industries. For example, in the deregulation I mentioned earlier, those of us industrialists who are afraid to jeopardize our vested interests are often to blame for keeping these regulations in place.

Current managers are exceptionally qualified for managing enterprises. Yet it may not be an exaggeration to say that we became managers without the basic philosophy that separates the ordinary manager from a true leader.

Government by Bureaucrats, Not by Law

Japan has yet to recover from the collapse of the "bubble economy." In fact, we have not seen the slightest signs of a recovery yet. I believe that the creation of this "bubble economy" and its collapse are due to the combined actions of bureaucrats and industrialists. The Diet is currently in turmoil over the settlement formula for the debts incurred by the housing loan companies, one of the negative legacies of the "bubble economy." The ruling party and the Ministry of Finance insist on using taxpayers' money to solve this problem, using the excuse that such a step is necessary in order to save the nation's financial system from collapse. However, it is a plan that completely flaunts existing rules. The fact that such actions are taken without the least hesitation is symptomatic of the evil brought about by our bureaucrat-led economic system.

If our companies should run into financial difficulties, we have no recourse other than to follow the methods prescribed by the law. That is our duty as law-abiding members of a country governed by law. No matter what the circumstances may be, it is abundantly clear that the government will not come to our rescue. We manage our companies on the assumption that there are strict rules in this market economy.

However, concerning the issue of the housing loan companies, the Ministry of Finance is taking a route that obviously should not exist in a country governed by law. And this is not the only instance. Similar actions by the bureaucrats can also be observed in the New York incident concerning Daiwa Bank. Ordinarily, when a major act of dishonesty and a huge loss are discovered in an enterprise, commercial law demands that such an incident be disclosed as soon as possible to protect shareholders. In this case, however, the disclosure was delayed for several months through the guidance of Japan's Ministry of Finance. The incident occurred in New York, but since Daiwa Bank was inveigled into this by the Japanese authorities, it is also a matter of grave concern for Japan as a whole.

The bad loans and overvalued assets held by Japan's financial institutions are said to be enormous. If an ordinary company were to have such bad debts, commercial law dictates that they would have to be disclosed at the end of the fiscal year. However, financial institutions under the jurisdiction of the Ministry of Finance are exempt from this requirement. When asked why, the Ministry of Finance answered that "if they were to fully disclose such a problem, the depositors might cause a run on the bank and financial instability could result." Yet disclosure of this information is a basic rule and principle of the free market economy. This is also an example of the evil brought about through the guidance of the Ministry of Finance, which ignores all accepted rules.

Whether as citizens or as managers, we are members of a constitutional state who must obey our laws and conduct our private and corporate lives accordingly. As stated in the Constitution, we believe all men are equal under the law. Laws are the basis of our society.

As I have shown, the current situation allows many issues to be arbitrarily decided by bureaucrats without regard to the laws in force. I am concerned that a society where such events are allowed to occur will someday become inevitably corrupted. The fact that the government takes measures outside the law confirms that Japan is not a constitutional state but only a bureaucratic dictatorship.

The Protection of Producers and Suppliers

The third salient feature of a bureaucratic dictatorship is that bureaucrats manage the nation by focusing rigidly on protecting and nurturing producers and suppliers, neglecting any effort to protect the interests of the average citizen and consumer. After the Meiji Restoration over a century ago, Japan made it a national strategy to catch up and surpass the developed nations of the West, at least in the areas of industrial and economic might. That became translated into the protection of producers and suppliers. Now, however, many Japanese companies have grown to the level where they are world-class enterprises, so there should no longer be any need for the government to protect and nurture producers and suppliers.

It is now time for us to shift our strategic direction to benefit the ordinary people, to permit them to lead truly affluent lives commensurate with the country's economic prosperity. Despite this, every government agency still sticks to the policy of protecting and nurturing producers and suppliers. For example, in the case of taxi cabs, even today restrictions prevent new companies from getting into the business. As a result, cab fares are increasing in every city. Another example is the new tariff structure that was recently introduced for

Japanese airlines, allowing them to determine air fares by themselves within a certain range specified by the government. Thus, the already high price of air fares rose even higher. However much the newspapers and other media point out such discrepancies and criticize them, the government shows no signs of discontinuing its policy of protecting industry.

Different opinions might be held on the subject of air fares, but no one can argue with the fact that the current low interest financial strategy has cut into the earnings of all pensioners and elderly people. This artificially low interest rate is allowing financial institutions to spend trillions upon trillions of yen to bail themselves out. This is surely a case of sacrificing the citizens for the sake of protecting industry.

The Selfishness of Private Corporations
It is not only our bureaucrats who are blame. We industrialists are just as guilty by thinking only of the interests of our own company or industry. A good example of this is the lifting of the prohibition on holding companies, whose principal business is to control the activities of a company or companies by means of holding stock. This deregulation is now under legislative consideration and is being enthusiastically promoted by members of Japan's economic circles.

Considering the very loose application of our antitrust regulations and the poor investigative resources of corporate shareholders, it is extremely dangerous to remove the restrictions we now have on holding companies and liberalize them to the level of those of Europe and the United States. I am afraid that we will have to pay a tremendous bill someday in the future if this deregulation is enacted. Before doing so, we should at least tighten the enforcement of Japan's antitrust laws to the level of Western nations.

I do not doubt that the industrialists in favor of lifting the ban on holding companies are doing so in good faith, but if there is no brake in the system, we may one day have an ambitious soul who will control a major corporation and pursue only his or her own profit, to the detriment of the nation and the people. I advocate being a lot more cautious to avoid this potential disaster.

There are many rumors concerning the deregulation of holding companies. One rumor has it that people from the financial world wish to deregulate merely to restructure their troubled financial institutions. Another rumor is that NTT, which is opposed to being split up like AT&T, is planning to use a holding company to effect a split-up in appearance only. I hope that these remain rumors, because if they are not, they reveal scandalous attitudes.

A Pragmatic Approach to Reform
To make Japan a truly livable country, bureaucrats should return to being "public servants." They should trust in the Japanese people, who have sovereign power, and they should promote strategies that will benefit and protect, most importantly, the citizen and consumer. We industrialists, too, need to have a management philosophy that can command the same respect as those of our predecessors; and we should try to promote social justice while considering the happiness of the ordinary citizen and respecting global friendship and harmony.

In other words, both bureaucrats and managers should switch their basic criterion for decision-making from egotism to altruism. I believe that such a shift could become the foundation for Japan's reform.

As I said earlier, Japan is unfortunately not yet truly democratic. In a real democracy, the nation is governed by the people and for the people, based on the concept that sovereignty rests with the people. However, Japan is governed by the bureaucrats for the bureaucrats, in a manner that can only be described as a bureaucratic dictatorship. For Japan to reform itself, we must first correct this system and make true democracy take root firmly. That means we have to construct a political system whereby our voices as citizens are reflected in government.

The people of present-day Japan are not the same as those in the unstable postwar period. We possess good common sense and good judgment. I think it is time to trust the people and listen to them about how our country should be governed.

Why has true democracy not yet taken root in Japan? One of the reasons is the attitude we industrialists have had toward politics. As managers, we have traditionally shied away from politics and kept our distance. We are worried that if we become interested or involved in politics, others will accuse us of wasting our time and neglecting our management duties. We are afraid that if we expend too much effort on politics, we'll neglect our responsibilities and lead our companies to failure. Another reason may be that we managers simply lack courage. If we were to lend support to one politician, we might incur the wrath of another, and one day that politician may take his revenge on our enterprise. Either of these reasons may underlie the fact that managers and salaried workers have tended to avoid any direct involvement in politics.

In fact, the only people who are involved in political activities in Japan appear to be labor union members who support left-wing agendas, general contractors who are interested in bidding for public construction projects, and certain religious groups. Yet if managers and professional workers were to become more interested in politics and use their votes to elect worthy political leaders, true democracy would take root more deeply and our government would be a better one.

The Kyoto Mayoral Election
I have learned my own lessons about avoiding direct involvement in politics. In February of this year, I had my first opportunity of becoming involved in an election—the campaign for the mayor of Kyoto. At that time, the issue of the housing loan companies had become the subject of bitter contention

between the governing and opposition parties in the Diet. It had also created a deadlock among the four coalition parties in the Kyoto City Council. As a completely neutral outsider, I was asked to be the campaign chairman for one of the candidates. I agreed to take on the task, thinking that I would merely be a figurehead.

However, as the governing factions were deadlocked, the opposing candidate from the Communist Party began to grow stronger by taking advantage of his local background and the housing loan companies scandal. Since I believed that the citizens of Kyoto would suffer if a communist mayor were elected, I decided to plunge wholeheartedly into campaigning.

I asked for the cooperation of Kyoto's business people, saying that "This is the time for us, business managers and employees, to have the courage to stand up for the people of Kyoto." They understood my intent and joined in the campaign. As a result, our candidate won—albeit by a slim margin of 4,000 votes.

From this experience, I gained confidence that if business managers and employees have enough courage to take action, we can elect candidates who are both capable and wise and can change things for the better. I learned that the most important aspect for the reform of Japan is to change our attitude toward politics.

Changing Japan's Political System
Currently, the Diet members with the highest number of re-elections take turns to become ministers of the different agencies. As soon as they have been selected for the post, they hold a press conference, saying words to the effect that "I did not expect to be selected for this ministerial position" and then simply repeating what they have been coached to say just hours earlier by the bureaucrats within their ministry. From then on, the new ministers are quite content to bask in the glory of their positions and let the bureaucrats conduct all the

day-to-day affairs of the ministry. This attitude, I believe, is what is corrupting the political system and giving rise to the bureaucratic dictatorship style of politics.

Japan's constitutional democracy should make it possible to elect candidates with excellent insight and judgment, candidates who can introduce changes to benefit the people at large. For each cabinet post, the prime minister should choose the most suitable person. Instead of merely following what the bureaucrats say, the ministers, together with their staff, should use their own knowledge and follow their consciences, and be courageous enough to reform the ministry and promote policies that benefit the public. If they cannot do this, their electorate should not elect them next time. True democracy, I believe, is essential in promoting Japan's reform.

However hard we may try, it is not possible for the bureaucrats to carry out the reforms I mentioned earlier. If we elect worthy politicians to head our ministries and if they are courageous enough carry out reforms following their consciences and good sense for the sake of their constituents, I am certain that Japan will become a better, more prosperous, and more humanistic nation.

In a few short years we will be entering the twenty-first century. Our predecessors managed to maintain their zeal and passion in order to rebuild Japan from the devastation of war. We should learn from them—now that it is our turn to be leaders—guided by altruism and the courage to bring about reforms and serve our fellow human beings.

Let us have courage. Let us take politics back into our own hands. Instead of being disinterested and uninvolved, let us elect outstanding politicians to the Diet to begin the reform of Japan. In this way, managers and business people can contribute to making Japan a truly wonderful nation that will be trusted and respected by other nations of the world.